DEVIL'S CHARGE

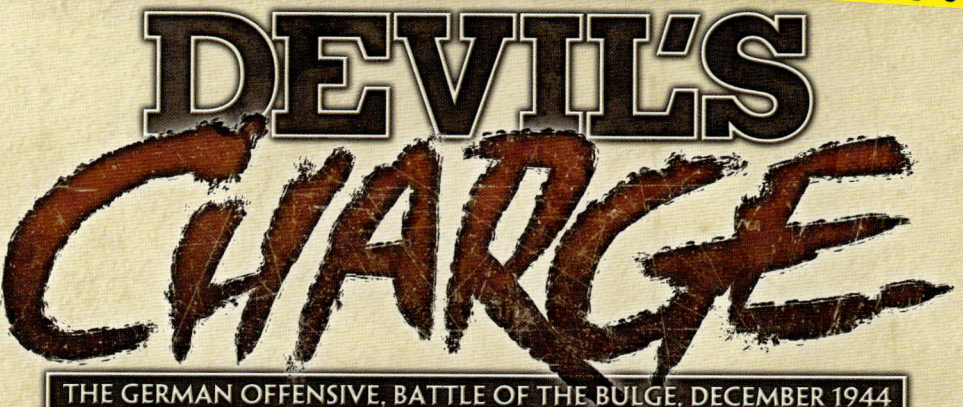

THE GERMAN OFFENSIVE, BATTLE OF THE BULGE, DECEMBER 1944

Written by: Michael Haught, Wayne Turner
Assistant Writer: Phil Yates
Editors: Peter Simunovich, John-Paul Brisigotti
Proof Readers: Russell Briant, Patrick Connolly, Joe Gallant, John Goetzinger, Bryan Koches, Gary Martin, Michael McSwiney, Gregg Siter, Neal Smith, Brian Wright
Graphic Design: Victor Pesch
Miniatures Design: Evan Allen, James Brown
Cover Art: Vincent Wai

Internal Art: Ben Wootten, Vincent Wai
Miniatures Painting: James Brown, Blake Coster, Thomas Crook, Mark Hazell, Aaron Mathie, Matt Parkes, Shelby Taylor
Terrain Modelling and Photography: Battlefront Studio
Playtest Groups: Dad's Army (Andrew Duncan), Einherjar (Gísli Jökull Gíslason), First Born Gaming (Charles McCall), Houston (Eric Warren), La Brigada de Madrid (Jorge Sancho), The Rat Patrol (Ed Leland), The Shed (Paul Turner), Spritz of War (Nicolò Da Lio)

CONTENTS

Wacht am Rhein (The Ardennes Offensive) 2	The Battle Babies, The 99th Infantry Division............... 42
Peiper's Charge.. 6	Viking Battalion, The 99th Infantry Battalion............. 44
SS-Kampfgruppe Peiper Special Rules 8	US Special Rules 45
Warrior: Jochen Peiper.................................. 9	Warrior: Audie Murphy................................... 46
SS-Kampfgruppe Peiper................................ 10	Rifle Company 48
German Support 15	The Damned Engineers!, The 291st Engineer Combat Battalion.. 56
Operation Griffin 18	Engineer Combat Company 58
Fielding Skorzeny Kommando Groups 20	Minding The Gap, The 14th Cavalry Group 62
150. Panzerbrigade Kampfgruppe................. 22	Cavalry Recon Troop..................................... 64
German Arsenal 28	Light Tank Company 66
Painting Guides 30	US Support 68
The Bloody Bucket, The 28th Infantry Division 34	US Arsenal 78
Perimeter Outpost... 36	Ardennes Battlefields.................................... 82
Indianheads, The 2nd Infantry Division 40	Winter Weather 84

This is a supplement for *Flames Of War*, the World War II miniatures game.
A copy of the rulebook for *Flames Of War* is necessary to fully use the contents of this book.

All rights reserved. No part of this publication may be reproduced, stored in a retrieval system, or transmitted, in any form or by any means without the prior written permission of the publisher, nor be otherwise circulated in any form of binding or cover other than that in which it is published and without a similar condition being imposed on the subsequent purchaser.

© Copyright BATTLEFRONT Miniatures Ltd., 2012. ISBN 978-0-9876609-5-4

WACHT AM RHEIN
THE ARDENNES OFFENSIVE

The autumn of 1944 presented Germany with a series of challenges. Major military setbacks in France and Byelorussia pushed the German army back to the Reich's frontier, Finland and Romania abandoned the Axis, and Allied bombers wrought havoc on German cities. Still, the German leader Adolf Hitler, was optimistic about winning the war with a grand winter offensive. In a meeting on 16 September, amidst gloomy reports from the front, Hitler sprang to his feet and declared, 'I have just made a momentous decision! I shall go over to the counterattack.' Pointing to the situation map he revealed his plan, '…out of the Ardennes, with the objective Antwerp.' His audience stood in amazement. Antwerp was 100 miles (160km) behind enemy lines. Could it be done? The *Führer* certainly thought so!

The obvious target for a counterattack was in the West, where the numbers of troops on each side were more balanced. The Allies had made headway in the Netherlands and in the Lorraine, leaving the space between, in the Ardennes Forest, lightly defended. A quick flanking victory through the Ardennes to Antwerp would trap three whole Allied armies and destroy a fourth in the process.

THE NORTHERN SHOULDER

The most critical objective, Antwerp, was given to Hitler's favourite army: *6. Panzerarmee* (Sixth Panzer Army) under the command of *SS-Oberstgruppenführer* (General) Josef Dietrich. The Germans attacked with nearly 5000 men on a small front, hoping to crack the untested US 99th Infantry Division. The infantry led the assault on 16 December after an artillery bombardment, and made some initial headway into the American lines. However, what the Germans hadn't counted on was just how close the veteran US 2nd Infantry Division was to the 99th and together the two American divisions stubbornly held the Germans at bay, first at the twin villages of Krinkelt and Rocherath, followed by an unbeatable defence of the Elsenborn Ridge. These two critical battles bought time for American reinforcements from the 1st and 30th Infantry and 82nd Airborne Divisions to arrive and finally halt the drive of the Sixth Panzer Army cold in its tracks. For victory, the Germans would have to look further south.

THE CENTRE COLLAPSES

As *6. Panzerarmee* attacked in the north, *5. Panzerarmee*, under the command of *General der Panzertruppe* (Lieutenant

THE ARDENNES

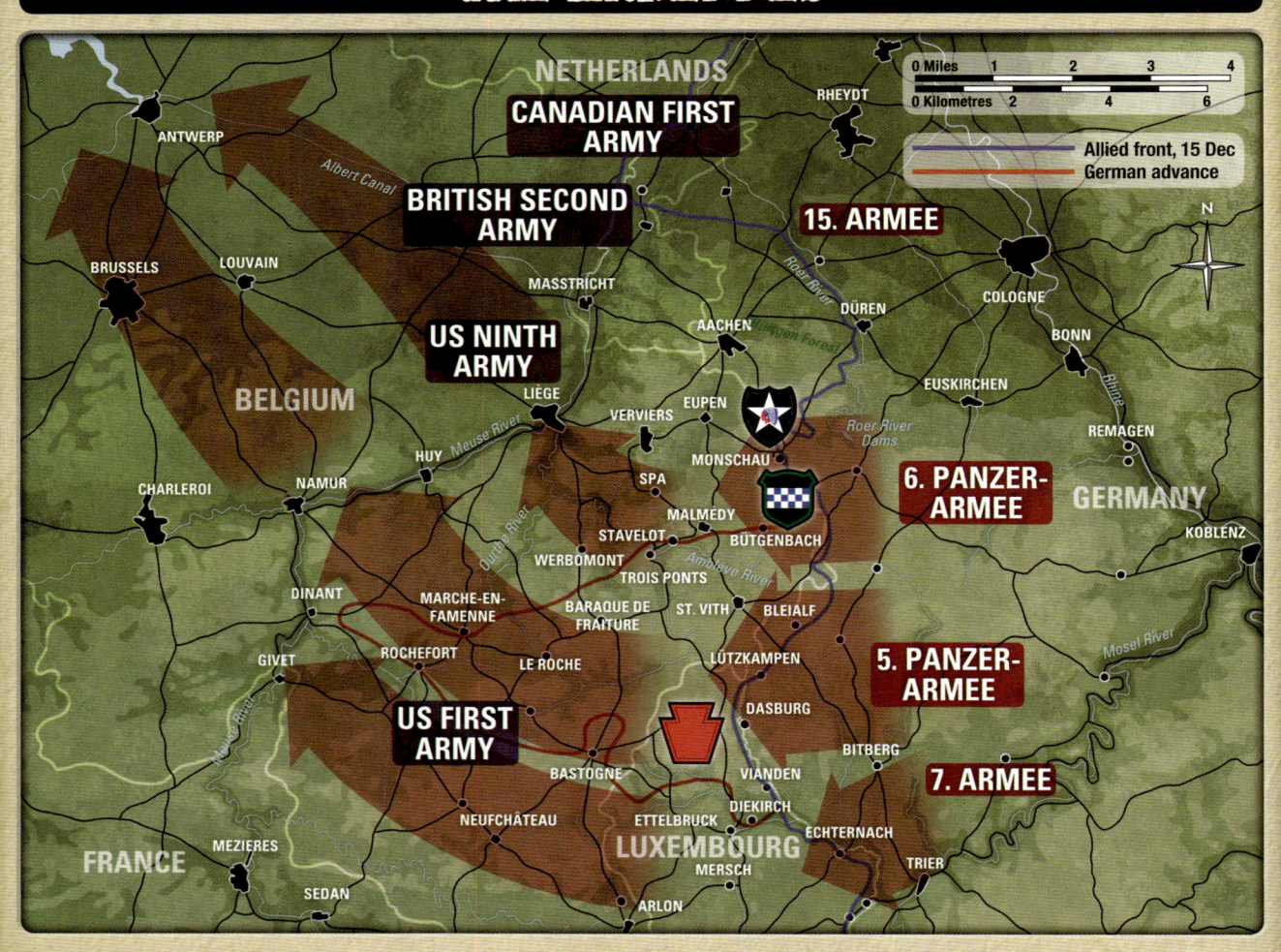

WACHT AM RHEIN

General) Hasso von Manteuffel, launched its assault against the American centre. Almost immediately, Manteuffel's achieved greater success than their comrades to the north. For start, they were lined up against the thinnest held portion of the US lines. Opposing them were only the 106th Infantry Division and a few elements of the 28th Infantry Division. The former was brand new and had only arrived in the Ardennes days before the attack. The latter was a worn-out division resting and awaiting replacements after a harrowing experience in the Hürtgen Forest the previous month. Between the two American divisions they had to hold over 30 miles (50km) of the front, but none of the Allied generals had anticipated an offensive in the area, so they figured the divisions were safe to rest and acclimatize themselves there.

When Manteuffel struck, the American divisions made some brave stands against the tide, but being so thinly deployed, it was hard to reinforce the front and the Germans were able to infiltrate between the American outposts. Before too long two of the 106th Infantry Division's regiments had been cut off and were forced to lay down arms. Over 8000 men were marched into captivity, the largest surrender of American troops since the Battle of Bataan in April 1942. With the 106th shattered, the men of the 28th stood little chance as their flank gave way. Still the outposts held firm for many critical hours, making it difficult for the infiltrating Germans to supply their spearheads. Gradually the battered 28th withdrew to Bastogne and then to the Meuse before collecting its scattered survivors and reforming.

One of the prizes in the centre was St. Vith. Its control of the local road network made it an essential objective and both sides were keenly aware of its importance. As the centre gave way, American reinforcements were rushed to St. Vith as quickly as possible. The US 7th and 9th Armored Divisions bravely held up the Axis attack on the city until they were reluctantly forced to withdraw behind the safety of the 82nd Airborne Division. Still, the bold and aggressive defence of the city bought the Allies enough time to help stabilise the centre and helping to prevent the German Fifth Panzer Army from reaching the Meuse.

The Southern Shoulder

The defence of the southern shoulder, with its critical crossings over the Our River and the important road junction at Bastogne, fell to the bulk of the 28th Infantry Division as well as their fellow Hürtgen Forest comrades, the 4th Infantry Division. Both had taken a beating in the November campaigns and both had been on the front lines since Normandy. Since the Allied high command had not expected any major offensives by the Germans, the Ardennes, with its hot spas and recreational facilities, was chosen to rest their weary divisions. The Americans fell into a quiet routine and worked on improving their winter quarters and outposts, taking up portions of the Germans' own Siegfried Line and integrating those defences into their perimeter.

On the German side, the Seventh Army, under the command of *General der Panzertruppe* Erich Brandenberger, had the task of securing the whole operation's southern flank, sweeping north from the Luxembourg frontier. Unlike the other two armies, Brandenberger's force was made up entirely of four infantry divisions and had no large tank formations under command. Still, Brandenberger was expected to attack alongside his comrades to the north.

On 16 December, the Seventh Army attacked, but all of his forces quickly became mired in bloody combat with the experienced troops of the 28th and 4th Infantry Divisions. The only real headway into the American lines was accomplished by the *5. Fallschirmjägerdivision* (5th Paratrooper Division) and that victory came at a high cost as the men of the 28th made them pay for every inch they gained. As the 28th was forced to withdraw, the 4th stood firm, forming the bottom of the rapidly-forming bulge in the American lines.

Brandenberger's advances near Bastogne owed everything to Manteuffel's success further north. Regardless, the Germans were now bearing down on that important road junction and the story of the Battle of the Bulge was about to reach its climax. All across the front, the German spearheads were being halted by tough American defenders, but the battle was far from over.

THE GERMANS ATTACK

Panther G tanks and SS-Panzergrenadiers of *SS-Kampfgruppe Peiper* clash with American Riflemen!

Ersatz StuG G assault guns, mocked-up to look like M7 Priests, move through a crossroads on to the next objective.

Fallschirmjäger supported by a *Königstiger* heavy tank probe through a town on their way to the next objective.

As the Germans advanced it began to snow. Peiper's Tiger and Panther tanks attack a US perimeter outpost.

Ersatz Panther tanks disguised as American M10 tank destroyers cross one of the many bridges in the Ardennes.

PEIPER'S CHARGE

On 11 December, *SS-Obersturmbannführer* (Lieutenant Colonel) Jochen Peiper was asked whether, if the roads were clear, could he cover 80km (50 miles) with his regiment in a single night. Rather than commit to an answer straight away, Peiper jumped into a Panther tank and put it to the test behind the German lines. He achieved the goal, but cautioned that moving a regiment was going to be more difficult than moving a single Panther through friendly territory. Three days later Peiper and his regiment became the spearhead *Kampfgruppe* (Battlegroup) of *Wacht Am Rhein* (Watch on the Rhine), the German offensive through the Ardennes.

SS-Kampfgruppe Peiper was formed around Peiper's *1. SS-Panzerregiment* (1st SS-Panzer Regiment). His regiment was short of tanks, so the heavy *Königstiger* (King Tiger) tanks of the *502. Schwere SS-Panzer Abteilung* (502nd Heavy SS-Panzer Battalion) were attached to his regiment. The battlegroup's mission was to exploit a gap to be made by *12. Volksgrenadierdivision* (12th People's Infantry Division) troops and head straight for the Meuse River with all due haste.

O-TAG (O-DAY)

On 16 December, Peiper travelled to the front to oversee the progress of the *Volksgrenadiere*, but he left disappointed as the infantry struggled to make any headway. Peiper then shifted his regiment south behind the *3. Fallschirmjägerdivision* (3rd Paratrooper Division) where a small breakthrough had been made at Lanzerath. When he arrived at around midnight Peiper found the *Fallschirmjäger* idle. He was furious that they weren't attacking and ordered a battalion of the paratroopers to be immediately attached to his unit.

The *Kampfgruppe* entered Büllingen unopposed and captured 50,000 gallons of fuel for their thirsty tanks. From there, Peiper turned south toward Möderscheid where the narrow roads suddenly became very difficult going due to the mud, so he redirected his regiment north to Faymonville.

STAVELOT

Peiper then pushed his troops on to Stavelot where he hoped to win a crossing over the Amblève River. Only the town's stone bridge could support the weight of his tanks, so that was the focus of the attack. The Germans launched a hasty assault on the bridge, but were stopped by a roadblock established by the 291st Engineer Combat Battalion. The following morning, Peiper charged into Stavelot with the full weight of his *Kampfgruppe*, quickly overrunning the bridge and bypassing the American defenders there.

TROIS PONTS

With this first major crossing complete, Peiper charged to the next crossing at Trois Ponts. This crossing was a bit trickier due as the town lay on both the Amblève and Salm Rivers. Peiper would need to capture several crossings to make it

PEIPER'S CHARGE: 16-25 DECEMBER

18 20 December, Midday-2000 hours: US Task Force Harrison (119th Infantry Regiment and 740th Tank Battalion, 30th Div) strikes Peiper's perimeter at the Stoumont Saint-Edouard Sanatorium. The building trades hands several times, but after the bloody fight, the Germans retain control.

19 20-21 December: The US 504th Parachute Infantry Regiment (82nd Airborne Division) attacks Cheneux. By nightfall, after a bloody fight the paratroopers only manage to grab a toehold in the town, only taking the rest on the following day.

20 20 December: US Task Force Lovelady (from the 3rd Armored Division) severs the road to Stavelot attacking Germans near Trois Ponts with the 505th Parachute Infantry Regiment (82nd Airborne). The task force moves on and links up with the Stavelot defenders, ending German hopes of reinforcing Peiper.

21 21 December: Despite being outnumbered, low on ammo, fuel, and food, Peiper staves off several US attempts to take Stoumont and La Gleize. On 21 December, Peiper withdraws from Stoumont to consolidate his lines at La Gleize.

22 24 December: At 1700 hours 23 December, Peiper is granted permission to break out of the encirclement. Leaving a small rearguard force to hold off the Americans, Peiper's group withdraws at 0200 hours on 24 December.

15 19 December, Morning: SS-Kampfgruppe Knittel, the 1. SS-Panzerdivision's reconnaissance battalion, joins Peiper at La Gleize.

16 19 December, 0900-1100 hours: Peiper attacks Stoumont. After a fierce battle, Peiper wins the town, but supplies have run out and Peiper is forced on the defensive.

17 19 December, 2100 hours: Peiper pulls back and forms a perimeter around Stoumont, Cheneux, and La Gleize.

13 18 December, 1400-1600 hours: A massive air attack strikes the column stretched along a 30km (19 miles) piece of the road. Peiper's Wirbelwind anti-aircraft tanks knock down several P-47 fighters for the loss of two Panther tanks and a few other vehicles.

14 18 December, 1430 hours: The nearby air attack alerts the engineers in Habiémont of Peiper's objectives and the bridge is blown. Peiper turns back to La Gleize.

PEIPER'S CHARGE

through. Splitting his force into two parts, Peiper led the main assault on Trois Ponts from the northern bank of the Amblève. The second attack was made by his light Panzer IV tanks and some panzergrenadiers from the eastern river bank. As both assaults neared their target, the engineers blew the bridges and stymied Peiper's attack. Frustrated, Peiper moved north along the Salm River until he found an unguarded crossing at Cheneux near the village of La Gleize.

From Cheneux he pressed on to Habiémont. En route the 30km-long column was hit by a massive air strike from three US fighter groups. Peiper only lost a few armoured vehicles, but the noise alerted the American engineers in Habiémont. As Peiper approached, the bridge was blown right in front of him. He banged his fist on his tank and exclaimed, 'Those damned engineers!'

STOUMONT

Peiper fell back to La Gleize and detoured to Stoumont. However, while Peiper was moving on Habiémont, the US 30th Infantry Division had arrived in Stoumont and a small task force of infantry, anti-tank guns, and a pair of 90mm heavy anti-aircraft guns were hastily set up to receive the Germans. A fierce fight broke out on the morning of 19 December. Five panzers were lost in the battle, but the German infantry overwhelmed the defenders and soon the town was in their hands.

The 30th Infantry counterattacked, backed by Sherman tanks and M36 tank destroyers. The two forces fought a bloody see-saw battle over Stoumont, but by nightfall neither force had complete control of the village.

TRAPPED

To make matters worse, the morning of 20 December, a powerful combat command from the US 3rd Armored Division hit Peiper in three places, blocking his northern flank, cutting Peiper's supply route to the rear, and flooding Stoumont with reinforcements. Meanwhile the 504th Parachute Infantry Regiment of the 82nd Airborne had arrived and put pressure on Peiper's southern flank at Cheneux, completing the encirclement on 21 December.

LA GLEIZE

Surrounded and unable to hold both Stoumont and La Gleize, Peiper fell back to the latter and set up a defensive perimeter. The rest of the Sixth Panzer Army tried to reach him, with *9. SS-Panzerdivision* and *1. SS-Panzerdivision*, but they were staunchly resisted by US tankers and paratroopers.

Peiper's troops defended La Gleize from several attempts by the 30th Infantry and 3rd Armored to push them out. The group's King Tigers proved their value in La Gleize, easily seeing off several attacks by Sherman medium tanks.

BREAKOUT

Now completely out of fuel and food, on 23 December Peiper decided to make a break out attempt on foot. Leaving a rearguard of skeleton crews to man the group's immobile tanks, Peiper's men disabled what they could, grabbed their hand weapons and slipped through the American cordon. The 800 survivors braved freezing weather and capture by American patrols before successfully reaching safety on the morning of 25 December.

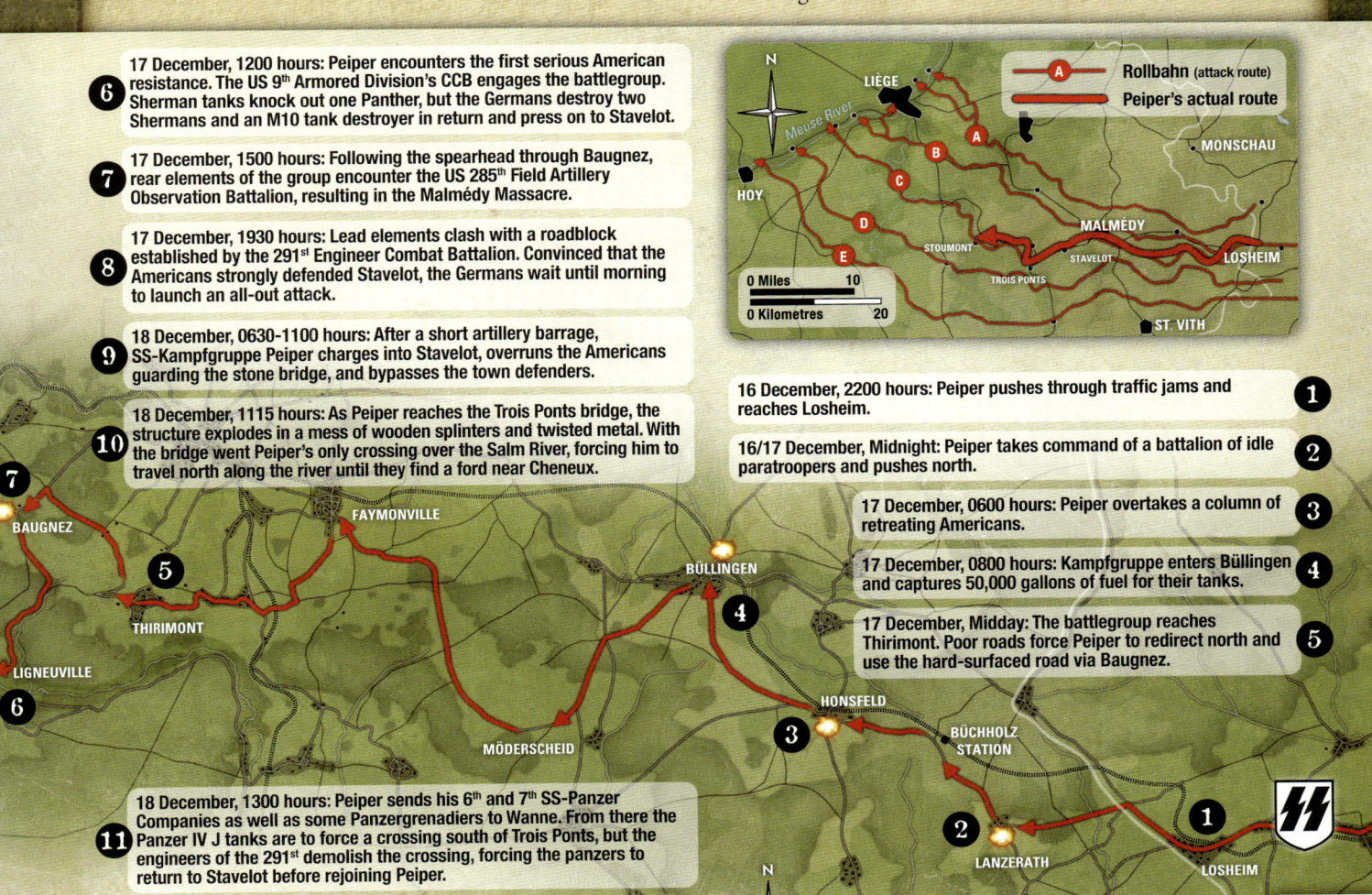

---

6 17 December, 1200 hours: Peiper encounters the first serious American resistance. The US 9th Armored Division's CCB engages the battlegroup. Sherman tanks knock out one Panther, but the Germans destroy two Shermans and an M10 tank destroyer in return and press on to Stavelot.

7 17 December, 1500 hours: Following the spearhead through Baugnez, rear elements of the group encounter the US 285th Field Artillery Observation Battalion, resulting in the Malmédy Massacre.

8 17 December, 1930 hours: Lead elements clash with a roadblock established by the 291st Engineer Combat Battalion. Convinced that the Americans strongly defended Stavelot, the Germans wait until morning to launch an all-out attack.

9 18 December, 0630-1100 hours: After a short artillery barrage, SS-Kampfgruppe Peiper charges into Stavelot, overruns the Americans guarding the stone bridge, and bypasses the town defenders.

10 18 December, 1115 hours: As Peiper reaches the Trois Ponts bridge, the structure explodes in a mess of wooden splinters and twisted metal. With the bridge went Peiper's only crossing over the Salm River, forcing him to travel north along the river until they find a ford near Cheneux.

11 18 December, 1300 hours: Peiper sends his 6th and 7th SS-Panzer Companies as well as some Panzergrenadiers to Wanne. From there the Panzer IV J tanks are to force a crossing south of Trois Ponts, but the engineers of the 291st demolish the crossing, forcing the panzers to return to Stavelot before rejoining Peiper.

12 18 December, 1400 hours: Peiper crosses the Salm River at Cheneux and leaves a detachment of 84. Flaksturmabteilung to guard the critical crossing.

---

1 16 December, 2200 hours: Peiper pushes through traffic jams and reaches Losheim.

2 16/17 December, Midnight: Peiper takes command of a battalion of idle paratroopers and pushes north.

3 17 December, 0600 hours: Peiper overtakes a column of retreating Americans.

4 17 December, 0800 hours: Kampfgruppe enters Büllingen and captures 50,000 gallons of fuel for his tanks.

5 17 December, Midday: The battlegroup reaches Thirimont. Poor roads force Peiper to redirect north and use the hard-surfaced road via Baugnez.

SS-Kampfgruppe Peiper

- 1. SS-Panzerkompanie
- 1. Schwere SS-Panzerkompanie
- 9. SS-Panzergrenadierkompanie
- 4. SS-Artillerie-Batterie
- 2. SS-Panzerkompanie
- 2. Schwere SS-Panzerkompanie
- 10. SS-Panzergrenadierkompanie
- 5. SS-Artillerie-Batterie
- 6. SS-Panzerkompanie
- 3. Schwere SS-Panzerkompanie
- 11. SS-Panzergrenadierkompanie
- 6. SS-Artillerie-Batterie
- 7. SS-Panzerkompanie
- 12. Schwere SS-Panzergrenadierkompanie
- 3. SS-Panzerpionier-Kompanie
- 9. SS-Panzerpionier-Kompanie
- 13. Schwere SS-Infanterie-Geschützkompanie
- 84. Flaksturm-Abteilung
- 10. SS-Panzerflak-Kompanie

SS-Kampfgruppe Peiper Special Rules

SS-Kampfgruppe Peiper uses all of the normal German special rules found on pages 241 to 245 of the rulebook. In addition, it also uses the following special rules.

Concerted Effort

During the Ardennes offensive the *Heer*, *Waffen-SS*, and *Luftwaffe* ground troops all worked together in a concerted effort to break through the US lines and push them back towards France. With the enemy at the doorstep of the Reich the petty squabbles of earlier years have faded into insignificance.

Luftwaffe and SS platoons in a SS-Kampfgruppe Peiper company ignore the Reich Divided rule (see page 242 of the rulebook) and therefore do not treat each other as Allies.

Peiper's Charge

Once *SS-Kampfgruppe Peiper* was free of traffic jams in Losheim, Peiper used his Panzer IV tanks and armoured infantry to lead the way through the American lines.

A player commanding SS-Kampfgruppe Peiper may elect to use the Always Attacks rule on page 257 of the rulebook.

If they do so, they may make a Spearhead Deployment (see page 261 in the rulebook) with any or all of their Gepanzerte SS-Panzergrenadier Platoons (including attached teams) and SS-Panzer Platoons equipped with Panzer IV J tanks.

SS-OBERSTURMBANNFÜHRER JOCHEN PEIPER

"My men are the products of total war … the only thing they knew was to handle weapons for the Reich…"

Jochen Peiper joined the *Leibstandarte SS Adolf Hitler* (*LSSAH*, Hitler's personal bodyguard) in 1936 and quickly rose through the ranks to become an adjutant to *Reichsführer-SS* Heinrich Himmler, the leader of the *Waffen-SS*, in 1938.

In 1940, Peiper was given leave to command an infantry company in France. After returning to Himmler's staff in June, he left once again to command his company during Operation Barbarossa, the invasion of the Soviet Union, where he earned a reputation as an aggressive combat leader.

When *LSSAH* was reformed as a *panzergrenadier* division in 1942, Peiper was given command of a battalion of armoured infantry. Peiper's men went into action at Kharkov, where under his aggressive leadership, they rescued an encircled infantry division. For his actions, he was promoted to *SS-Obersturmbannführer* (Lieutenant Colonel) and given command of the *1. SS-Panzerregiment* (1st SS-Panzer Regiment).

In December 1944, Peiper led his regiment during the Ardennes Offensive. His aggressive command made him an ideal candidate to spearhead the assault of *LSSAH*. During his drive to the Meuse, Peiper never lost sight of the objective, and when a problem asserted itself he lost no time in coming up with a solution. When he could go no further, Peiper put the welfare of his men ahead of victory and led them to safety during a harrowing escape on foot through snow and ice.

However, for all of his achievements, his reputation was forever marred by the incidents surrounding the Malmédy Massacre. After the war, Peiper was brought up on charges of war crimes he committed in Russia, Italy, and Belgium. Although found guilty, his death sentence was commuted to an 11-year imprisonment term. On release, he then moved to France where he was killed by French communists after a gunfight at his home in 1976.

CHARACTERISTICS

SS-Obersturmbannführer Jochen Peiper is a Warrior Higher Command Tank Team rated **Fearless Veteran**. He may join an *SS-Kampfgruppe* Peiper company (page 10) mounted in his own Panther G tank for +235 points

TO THE MEUSE!

Peiper's battlegroup might have been small, but he used it with precision and skill. He knew when to pull his troops together to overcome American strongpoints and counter-attacks and, when he could afford to, split his forces to cover more ground and find suitable crossings.

Once each turn, you may re-roll one die when rolling for Reserves.

In a mission using the Scattered Reserves special rule, once per turn you may also re-roll one die rolled to determine where a platoon will arrive from Scattered Reserve.

SS-KAMPFGRUPPE PEIPER
BATTLE GROUP PEIPER
TANK COMPANY

Motivation and Skill

Even as the rest of the German army has begun scraping the bottom of the barrel for personnel, the SS has had no problem filling their ranks with motivated, if inexperienced, recruits. SS-Kampfgruppe Peiper is rated **Fearless Trained**.

RELUCTANT	CONSCRIPT
CONFIDENT	**TRAINED**
FEARLESS	VETERAN

HEADQUARTERS
- SS-Kampfgruppe Peiper HQ — 11

You must field one platoon from each box shaded black and may field one platoon from each box shaded grey.

COMBAT PLATOONS

ARMOUR
- SS-Panzer Platoon — 11
- Schwere SS-Panzer Platoon — 12

ARMOUR OR INFANTRY
- SS-Panzer Platoon — 11
- Schwere SS-Panzer Platoon — 12
- Gepanzerte SS-Panzegrenadier Platoon — 12

ARMOUR OR INFANTRY
- SS-Panzer Platoon — 11
- Schwere SS-Panzer Platoon — 12
- Gepanzerte SS-Panzegrenadier Platoon — 12

WEAPONS PLATOONS

ANTI-AIRCRAFT
- SS-Panzer Anti-aircraft Gun Platoon — 13

MACHINE-GUNS
- SS-Panzergrenadier Heavy Platoon — 13

ARTILLERY
- SS-Heavy Mortar Platoon — 14
- SS-Cannon Platoon — 14

Remember, Luftwaffe and SS platoons in a SS-Kampfgruppe Peiper force ignore the Reich Divided rule.

SUPPORT PLATOONS

INFANTRY
- Gepanzerte SS-Panzergrenadier Platoon — 12
- SS-Panzerpionier Platoon — 15
- Fallschirmjäger Platoon — 17

INFANTRY
- SS-Panzerpionier Platoon — 15
- Fallschirmjäger Platoon — 17

RECONNAISSANCE
- Skorzeny Commando Group — 20
- SS-Panzerspäh Platoon — 17

ARTILLERY
- SS-Artillery Battery — 16

ARTILLERY
- SS-Self-propelled Infantry Gun Battery — 16

ANTI-AIRCRAFT
- Luftwaffe Anti-aircraft Gun Platoon — 17

ANTI-AIRCRAFT
- Luftwaffe Anti-aircraft Gun Platoon — 17

AIRCRAFT
- Air Support — 15

SS-KAMPFGRUPPE PEIPER

HEADQUARTERS

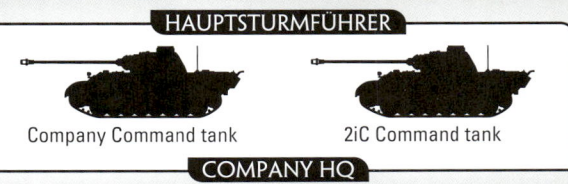

SS-Kampfgruppe Peiper HQ

Headquarters

2 Panzer IV J	150 points
1 Panzer IV J	75 points
2 Panther G	325 points
1 Panther G	165 points
2 Königstiger (Henschel)	600 points
1 Königstiger (Henschel)	305 points

A Company Command Königstiger tank always has two Tiger Ace Skills (see page 244 of the rule book).

At least one of your Combat Platoons must be equipped with the same type of tank as your Company HQ.

COMBAT PLATOONS

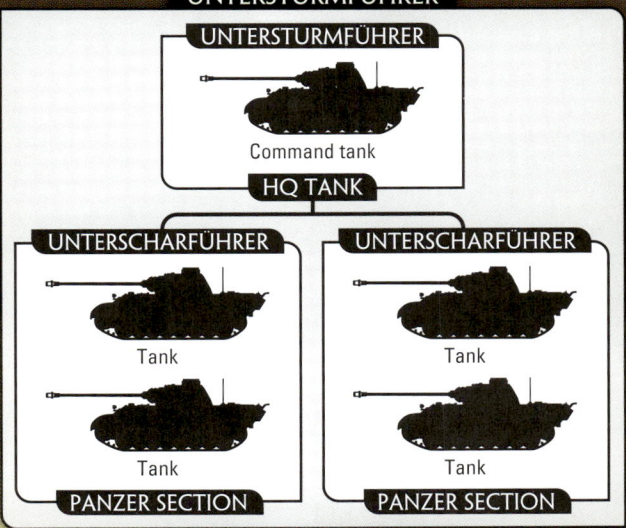

SS-Panzer Platoon

Platoon

5 Panzer IV J	375 points
4 Panzer IV J	300 points
3 Panzer IV J	225 points
5 Panther G	815 points
4 Panther G	655 points
3 Panther G	490 points

1. SS-Panzerkompanie and *2. SS-Panzerkompanie* were equipped with excellent Panther tanks. However, Peiper placed the greatest responsibilities on the *6. SS-Panzerkompanie* and *7. SS-Panzerkompanie* and their trusty Panzer IV J tanks. These smaller tanks could navigate the narrow and muddy roads much better than the heavier Panthers and only used a fraction of the fuel.

Schwere SS-Panzer Platoon
Platoon

4 Königstiger (Henschel)	1180 points
3 Königstiger (Henschel)	885 points
2 Königstiger (Henschel)	590 points
1 Königstiger (Henschel)	295 points

Remember to roll for your Tiger Ace Skills before each game (see page 244 of the rule book).

Peiper's regiment was reinforced by the *502. SS-Schwere Panzer Abteilung* (502nd SS-Heavy Panzer Battalion). This battalion was equipped with the *Königstiger*, or King Tiger. Their slow speed and bulk placed them at the end of Peiper's column at the start, but when they began to encounter strong American counterattacks, these nearly invincible beasts proved essential to the mission.

Gepanzerte SS-Panzergrenadier Platoon
Platoon

HQ Section with:

3 Panzergrenadier Squads	200 points
2 Panzergrenadier Squads	145 points

Option
- Replace the Command MG team with a Command Panzerfaust SMG team for +10 points. If you do this you may also replace all remaining MG teams in the platoon with Panzerfaust MG teams for +10 points per team.

A Gepanzerte SS-Panzergrenadier Platoon may use the Mounted Assault special rule (see page 243 of the rulebook).

Peiper integrated his armoured grenadiers among the tank platoons to offer immediate infantry support when needed.

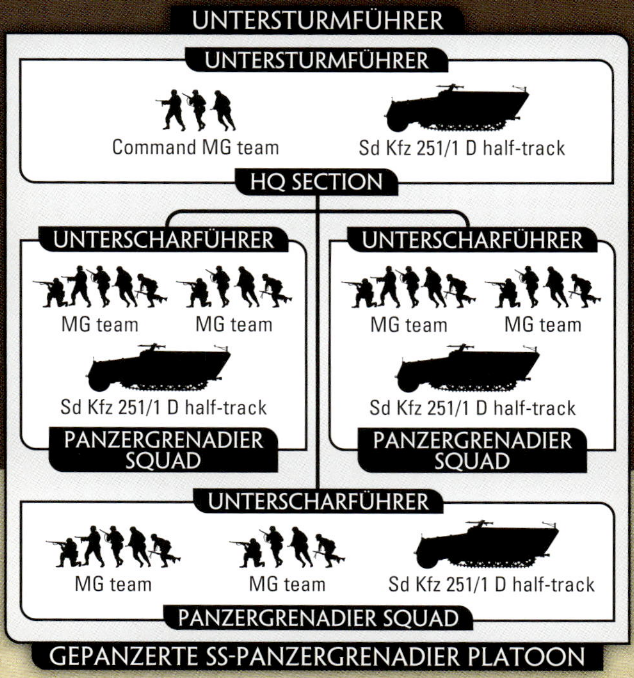

WEAPONS PLATOONS

SS-Panzergrenadier Heavy Platoon

Platoon

HQ Section with:

1 Machine-gun Section	205 points
No Machine-gun Section	15 points

Options

- Add Mortar Section for +75 points.
- Add Gun Section for +70 points.

An SS-Panzergrenadier Heavy Platoon must have a Mortar Section or Gun Section if it has no Machine-gun Section.

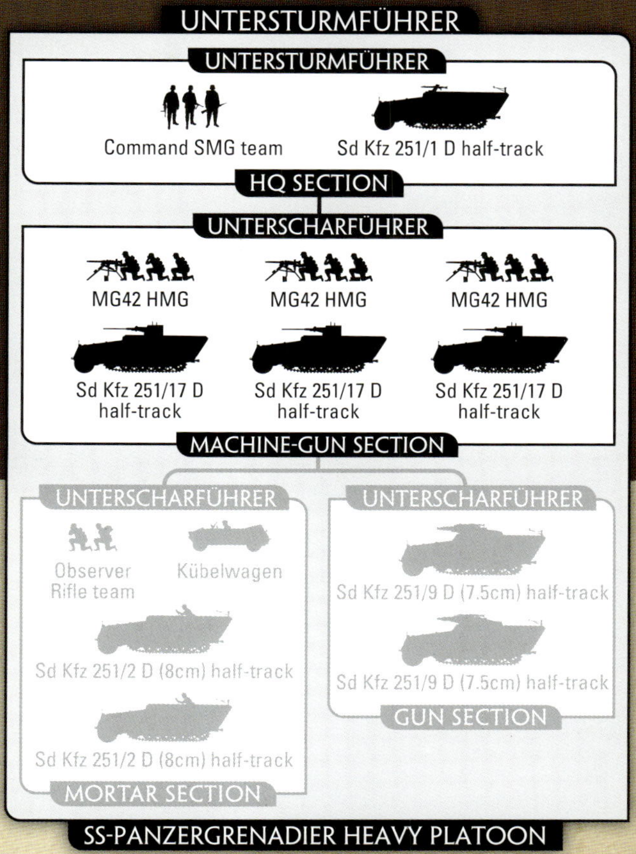

The HQ Section of the SS-Panzergrenadier Heavy Platoon uses the Mounted Assault special rule (see page 243 of the rulebook).

The SS-Panzergrenadier Heavy Platoon may make Combat Attachments to Gepanzerte SS-Panzergrenadier Platoons.

An Sd Kfz 251/17 D (2cm) half-track is a Tank team, but can carry one Passenger team as if it was a Transport team.

SS-PANZERGRENADIER HEAVY PLATOON

UNTERSTURMFÜHRER
- Command SMG team
- Sd Kfz 251/1 D half-track

HQ SECTION

UNTERSCHARFÜHRER
- MG42 HMG — Sd Kfz 251/17 D half-track
- MG42 HMG — Sd Kfz 251/17 D half-track
- MG42 HMG — Sd Kfz 251/17 D half-track

MACHINE-GUN SECTION

UNTERSCHARFÜHRER
- Observer Rifle team
- Kübelwagen
- Sd Kfz 251/2 D (8cm) half-track
- Sd Kfz 251/2 D (8cm) half-track

MORTAR SECTION

UNTERSCHARFÜHRER
- Sd Kfz 251/9 D (7.5cm) half-track
- Sd Kfz 251/9 D (7.5cm) half-track

GUN SECTION

SS-Panzer Anti-aircraft Gun Platoon

Platoon

4 Wirbelwind (Quad 2cm)	190 points
3 Wirbelwind (Quad 2cm)	140 points
2 Wirbelwind (Quad 2cm)	90 points
4 Möbelwagen (3.7cm)	190 points
3 Möbelwagen (3.7cm)	140 points
2 Möbelwagen (3.7cm)	90 points
4 Ostwind (3.7cm)	205 points
3 Ostwind (3.7cm)	155 points
2 Ostwind (3.7cm)	105 points

SS-PANZER ANTI-AIRCRAFT GUN PLATOON

UNTERSTURMFÜHRER
- Command Anti-aircraft tank
- Anti-aircraft tank

HQ SECTION

UNTERSCHARFÜHRER
- Anti-aircraft tank
- Anti-aircraft tank

ANTI-AIRCRAFT SECTION

The *Wirbelwind* (Whirlwind) and *Ostwind* (East Wind) anti-aircraft tanks provided essential cover from the frequent air attacks on the column, especially when three American fighter groups attacked together outside Cheneux.

SS-KAMPFGRUPPE PEIPER

SS-Heavy Mortar Platoon

Platoon

HQ Section with:

4 12cm sGW43	135 points

Options

- Add Sd Kfz 251/1 half-tracks and Kübelwagen jeep for +25 points for the platoon.
- Add up to two Sd Kfz 251/1 (Stuka) half-tracks for +35 points per half-track.

Each Sd Kfz 251/1 D (Stuka) half-track fires a bombardment completely separate from the rest of the SS-Heavy Mortar Platoon using the Stuka zu Fuss rules on page 245 of the rulebook. A Sd Kfz 251/1 D (Stuka) half-track cannot act as the Spotting team for the 12cm sGW43 mortars, nor can the mortars or the Observer team act as the Spotting team for a Sd Kfz 251/1 D (Stuka) half-track.

The heavy mortars from the *SS-Panzergrenadier* battalions offered quick and accurate artillery support to the column.

UNTERSTURMFÜHRER
- Command SMG team
- Sd Kfz 251/1 D half-track
- Observer Rifle team
- Kübelwagen

HQ SECTION

UNTERSCHARFÜHRER
- 12cm sGW43 mortar
- Sd Kfz 251/1 D half-track
- 12cm sGW43 mortar
- Sd Kfz 251/1 D half-track

UNTERSCHARFÜHRER
- 12cm sGW43 mortar
- Sd Kfz 251/1 D half-track
- 12cm sGW43 mortar
- Sd Kfz 251/1 D half-track

MORTAR SECTION

UNTERSCHARFÜHRER
- Sd Kfz 251/1 D (Stuka) half-track
- Sd Kfz 251/1 D (Stuka) half-track

LAUNCHER SECTION

SS-HEAVY MORTAR PLATOON

SS-Cannon Platoon

Platoon

6 Sd Kfz 251/9 (7.5cm)	210 points
4 Sd Kfz 251/9 (7.5cm)	140 points
2 Sd Kfz 251/9 (7.5cm)	70 points

One of the greatest challenges tankers face is dislodging dug-in infantry. Fortunately, the *SS-Panzergrenadiere* have several Sd Kfz 251/9 (7.5cm) assault guns. These free up the tanks to carry on exploiting breakthroughs while the infantry and assault guns get to work reducing enemy infantry outposts and roadblocks.

UNTERSTURMFÜHRER
- Command Sd Kfz 251/9 D (7.5cm) half-track
- Sd Kfz 251/9 D (7.5cm) half-track

GUN SECTION

UNTERSCHARFÜHRER
- Sd Kfz 251/9 D (7.5cm) half-track
- Sd Kfz 251/9 D (7.5cm) half-track

UNTERSCHARFÜHRER
- Sd Kfz 251/9 D (7.5cm) half-track
- Sd Kfz 251/9 D (7.5cm) half-track

GUN SECTION

SS-CANNON PLATOON

GERMAN SUPPORT

Motivation and Skill

The supporting troops in SS-Kampfgruppe Peiper were just as willing and able to fight as their comrades at the head of the column. SS-Panzerdivision support platoons are rated **Fearless Trained** unless otherwise noted.

RELUCTANT	CONSCRIPT
CONFIDENT	TRAINED
FEARLESS	VETERAN

AIR SUPPORT

Sporadic Air Support

Me 262 A2a Sturmvogel	105 points

High-speed Jet

Ground attacks by Me 262 A2a aircraft cannot be intercepted using the Fighter Interception rule on page 179 of the rulebook.

The *Luftwaffe* (German Air Force) was not idle over the skies of Belgium with fighter-bombers attacking targets of opportunity. However, it was also the debut of the world's first operational jet fighter: the Me 262. The ground attack version, the Me 262 A2a *Sturmvogel* (Storm Bird), was armed with two 30mm cannons and a pair of 250kg (550lb) bombs. Its excellent speed of 540mph (870km/h) meant that it could outrun any Allied fighter, making it impossible to catch.

LEUTNANT
LEUTNANT
Me 262 A2a Sturmvogel
FLIGHT
AIR SUPPORT

Operation Bodenplatte

Operation *Bodenplatte* (Baseplate) was to be launched on 16 December 1944. Its mission was to cripple Allied air support giving the ground units of *Wacht Am Rhein* a fighting chance. However, the weather refused to co-operate and the operation wasn't launched until 1 January 1945. Over 900 aircraft took to the skies and struck the Allies' air bases in Belgium and Holland and destroyed somewhere between 300 and 400 Allied aircraft. This success, however, came at the steep price of over 300 German aircraft.

SS-PANZERPIONIER PLATOON

Platoon

HQ Section with:

2 Pioneer Squads	175 points

Options

- Replace the Command Pioneer MG team with a Command Pioneer Panzerfaust SMG team for +10 points. If you do this you may also replace all remaining Pioneer MG teams in the platoon with Panzerfaust Pioneer MG teams for +10 points per team.
- Add an additional Sd Kfz 251/7 (Pioneer) half-track to each squad for +10 points per half-track.
- Add Pioneer Supply Maultier half-track for +30 points.

You may replace up to one Pioneer MG team or Panzerfaust Pioneer MG team per Pioneer Squad with a Flame-thrower team at the start of the game before deployment.

A Gepanzerte SS-Panzerpionier Platoon may use the Mounted Assault special rule (see page 243 of the rulebook).

UNTERSTURMFÜHRER
UNTERSTURMFÜHRER
Command Pioneer MG team — Sd Kfz 251/7 D half-track — Pioneer Supply Opel Maultier
HQ SECTION

UNTERSCHARFÜHRER | **UNTERSCHARFÜHRER**
Pioneer MG team — Sd Kfz 251/7 D half-track | Pioneer MG team — Sd Kfz 251/7 D half-track
Pioneer MG team — Sd Kfz 251/7 D half-track | Pioneer MG team — Sd Kfz 251/7 D half-track
PIONEER SQUAD | **PIONEER SQUAD**
SS-PANZERPIONEER PLATOON

Peiper's engineers were placed in the lead and rear of the column. The lead company (3. SS-Panzerpionierkompanie from the divisional pioneers) was available to clear mines and disarm American demolitions at the critical river crossings. The rear company (9. SS-Panzerpionierkompanie from his own panzer regiment) set about reconstructing demolished bridges and securing the column's supply route.

SS-Artillery Battery

Platoon

HQ Section with:

6 10.5cm leFH18/40	255 points
4 10.5cm leFH18/40	185 points
3 10.5cm leFH18/40	140 points
6 15cm sFH18	385 points
4 15cm sFH18	275 points
3 15cm sFH18	205 points

Options

- Add Kfz 15 field car, Kfz 68 radio truck, and 3-ton trucks to your battery equipped with 10.5cm leFH18/40 howitzers for +5 points for the battery.
- Add Kfz 15 field car, Kfz 68 radio truck, and Sd Kfz 7 half-tracks to your battery equipped with 15cm sFH18 howitzers for +5 points for the battery.

The *1. SS-Panzerartillerieregiment* (1st SS-Armoured Artillery Regiment) had two battalions of 10.5cm leFH18/40 light howitzers and one battalion of 15cm sFH18 heavy howitzers. Peiper used these to bombard Stavelot before he rushed the town's bridge.

SS-Self-propelled Infantry Gun Battery

Platoon

HQ Section with:

6 Grille (15cm sIG) K	365 points
4 Grille (15cm sIG) K	265 points
2 Grille (15cm sIG) K	145 points

The towed artillery was best used when the battlegroup had come to a stop, but since the mission was to get to the Meuse as fast as possible, Peiper opted to keep the entirety of his *13. SS Schwere Infanteriegeschützkompanie* (the panzergrenadiers' 13th SS Heavy Infantry Gun Company) together as a single mobile battery.

In Stoumont, Peiper deployed the company's six self-propelled guns in the southeastern corner of the village in a little clearing overlooking the area. From there the heavy shells of the battery helped break up the American attempts to seize the village.

GERMAN SUPPORT

SS-Panzerspäh Platoon

Platoon

3 Sd Kfz 234/1 (2cm)	110 points
3 Sd Kfz 234/2 (Puma)	130 points

An SS-Panzerspäh Platoon is a Reconnaissance Platoon.

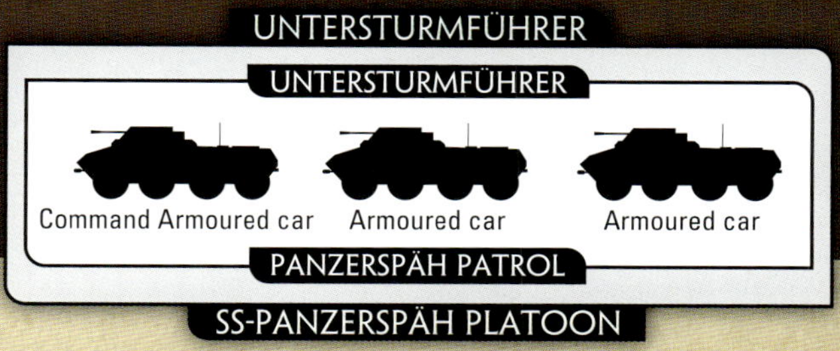

SS-PANZERSPÄH PLATOON
- UNTERSTURMFÜHRER
  - PANZERSPÄH PATROL
    - UNTERSTURMFÜHRER: Command Armoured car, Armoured car, Armoured car

Fallschirmjäger Platoon

Platoon

HQ Section with:

3 Fallschirmjäger Squads	205 points
2 Fallschirmjäger Squads	145 points

Option
- Replace the Command Rifle/MG team with a Command Panzerfaust SMG team for +10 points. If you do this you may also replace all remaining Rifle/MG teams in the platoon with Panzerfaust Rifle/MG teams for +10 points per team.

Tank Riders

Teams from a Fallschirmjäger Platoon have a 3+ Save while Mounted on Königstiger (Henschel) tanks as Passengers. They do not need to Dismount Under Fire when hit. They can remain on the tanks instead.

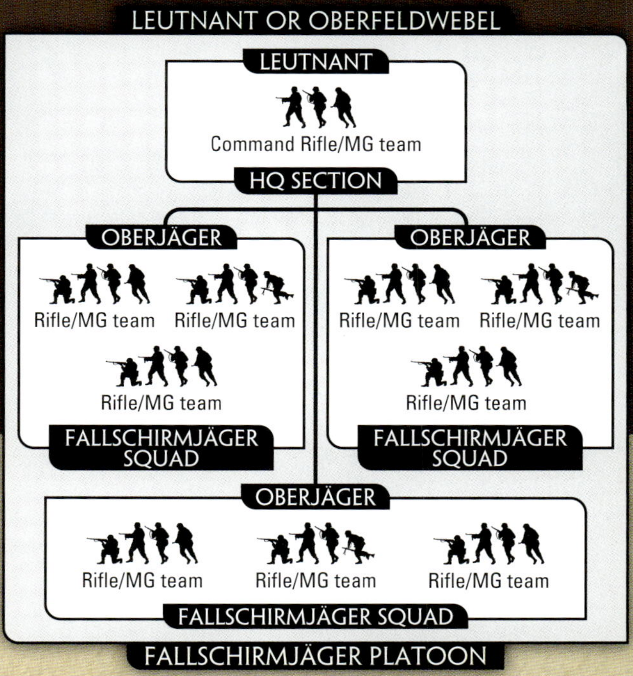

FALLSCHIRMJÄGER PLATOON
- LEUTNANT OR OBERFELDWEBEL
  - LEUTNANT — HQ SECTION: Command Rifle/MG team
  - OBERJÄGER — FALLSCHIRMJÄGER SQUAD: Rifle/MG team, Rifle/MG team, Rifle/MG team
  - OBERJÄGER — FALLSCHIRMJÄGER SQUAD: Rifle/MG team, Rifle/MG team, Rifle/MG team
  - OBERJÄGER — FALLSCHIRMJÄGER SQUAD: Rifle/MG team, Rifle/MG team, Rifle/MG team

Luftwaffe Anti-aircraft Gun Platoon

Platoon

3 Sd Kfz 10/5 (2cm)	60 points
3 Sd Kfz 7/1 (Quad 2cm)	85 points
3 Sd Kfz 7/2 (3.7cm)	95 points

A Luftwaffe Anti-aircraft Gun Platoon is rated **Reluctant Trained.**

RELUCTANT	TRAINED

LUFTWAFFE ANTI-AIRCRAFT GUN PLATOON
- LEUTNANT — ANTI-AIRCRAFT SECTION: Command Anti-aircraft gun
- UNTEROFFIZIER — AA SECTION: Anti-aircraft gun
- UNTEROFFIZIER — AA SECTION: Anti-aircraft gun

17

OPERATION GRIFFIN

No story of *Unternehmen Greif*, or Operation Griffin, would be complete without first looking at the man behind the plan: Otto Skorzeny. The charismatic six-foot, four-inch (1.93m) Austrian joined the *Waffen-SS* in 1939 and served in Holland, France, and the Balkans before he was badly wounded in Russia. While recovering he became interested in commando warfare and wrote up some proposals, which were met with enthusiasm. Soon Skorzeny was put in command of a special forces training facility. He quickly won fame after the wild success of *Unternehmen Eiche* (Operation Oak), where he and his commandos rescued the Italian dictator Benito Mussolini from Allied custody in September 1943. With that, he became a favourite of Hitler and was known to Allied intelligence as the most dangerous man in Europe.

UNTERNEHMEN GREIF

On 22 October 1944, Hitler brought Skorzeny up to speed on his new offensive and outlined how he wanted the commandos to help by using infiltration tactics, capturing bridges, and sowing confusion behind the lines. To help, Hitler wrote Skorzeny a general order authorising him whatever he needed for the mission.

Skorzeny crafted a plan based around two elements. The first was a commando unit known as *Einheit Stielau*. These men were drafted from the best American-English speakers under his command. Their role was to infiltrate the enemy and cause chaos behind the lines ahead of the main assault.

The second element was *150. Panzerbrigade* (150th Armoured Brigade). This was the military arm of the operation, intended to be entirely equipped with captured American vehicles, weapons, and uniforms. After the German assault waves opened a gap, *150. Panzerbrigade* would sneak through, capture critical bridges, and ultimately reach the Meuse, relying on their disguises to pass as American troops.

FILLING THE RANKS

Skorzeny used his blank cheque from Hitler to order all German units to send him their captured weapons, uniforms, and vehicles of American origin. What he received was a wide assortment of equipment that fell seriously short of what he needed. For example, he didn't have any operable American tanks other than a few armoured cars. To make up the numbers, Skorzeny acquired five Panther tanks, five StuG G assault guns, and six German armoured cars, with the crews supplied from experienced *Heer* (Army) units. He also received elite infantry from the *Luftwaffe* (Air Force), *Waffen-SS*, and the famed *Grossdeutschland* Division. Skorzeny's workshop engineers converted the German-made tanks to resemble American ones. His Panthers were altered to look like American M10 tank destroyers and the StuG assault guns to look like M7 Priests (at least that's the best guess, as the conversion wasn't very successful). All of the unit's vehicles, including the German ones, were painted green and large white stars were displayed on the sides, front, and top. The disguises weren't fool-proof, but at least the brigade was ready for combat.

COMMANDO OPERATIONS

On the eve of the offensive, the commandos were split into numerous groups. Each of the divisions leading the attack in the Sixth Panzer Army sector, including Peiper's *Kampfgruppe*, was assigned a commando group, while three groups were assigned to support *150. Panzerbrigade* directly. The rest were turned loose to do what they could. The commandos issued false orders, reversed road signs, moved minefield warning signs, severed telephone communications, and spread rumours to cause panic among the Americans.

For the small number of men involved, the commandos caused an impressive amount of confusion. American soldiers as far south as Patton's Third Army over 50 miles (80km) away were seeing the enemy in every unfamiliar face. Overcautious military police arrested everyone who failed to answer simple questions they assumed all Americans would know. In fact, when challenged by an infantryman, Brigadier General Bruce Clarke of the 7th Armored Division insisted that the Chicago Cubs baseball team was part of the American League. It turns out he was wrong and he was arrested as a spy and detained for a short while.

Despite these measures, in the end only eight of the 44 commandos sent across the line were captured. Those that fell into American hands faced the firing squad for wearing the enemy's uniform, but before the sentence was carried out, these prisoners boasted about extravagant assassination plans.

This last act of deception would have the Allies place in protective custody their own political leaders, even General Eisenhower himself, for days until the threat had passed.

Kampfgruppen X, Y, & Z

150. Panzerbrigade was split up into three battlegroups, named X, Y, and Z. Like the commandos, these were attached to the assault divisions in the Sixth Panzer Army. However, when the offensive stalled, Skorzeny realized that his opportunity was lost. He received permission to abandon his plans and bring his unit together to fight as a regular unit and help get the offensive going again.

Malmédy

On 18 December, Skorzeny was ordered to take Malmédy to secure Peiper's northern flank. His commandos reported that the town was thinly held by the 291st Combat Engineer Battalion and open for the taking. Once the brigade had assembled on 21 December, Skorzeny attacked. However, in the three days between the commandos' report and the attack, the engineers in Malmédy had been reinforced by infantry, towed tank destroyers, and two 90mm heavy anti-aircraft guns.

To test the American defences, Skorzeny attacked with *Kampfgruppe Y* from the east, with its infantry and StuG assault guns. The group met fierce resistance from American outposts and artillery and broke off their attack.

Kampfgruppe X had better luck when they hit the western side of the town. A large railway viaduct crossed the battlefield, from which the Americans opened fire. The Germans slowly pushed on under the murderous fire with the help of the Panthers and trapped 30 men in a house. A brutal fight for the house broke out as the grenadiers fought the GIs inside. The Panthers bypassed the house and within minutes several Panthers were knocked out by 90mm anti-aircraft guns and tank destroyers, forcing *Kampfgruppe X* back.

Finally at 1400hrs on 22 December, the Engineers demolished the Malmédy bridge. With that the town was no longer a German priority and Skorzeny's brigade withdrew. *150. Panzerbrigade* fought on until 23 January 1945 when it was finally disbanded and all of its members returned to their original units.

150. PANZERBRIGADE SPECIAL RULES

A *150. Panzerbrigade Kampfgruppe* uses all of the normal German special rules found on pages 241 to 245 of the rulebook. In addition they also use the Concerted Effort and Enemy Disguises special rules below, and the Skorzeny Commando Groups special rules on page 20.

Concerted Effort

During the Ardennes offensive the *Heer*, *SS*, and *Luftwaffe* ground troops all worked together in a concerted effort to break through the US lines and push them back towards France. With the enemy at the doorstep of the Reich, the petty squabbles of earlier years have faded into insignificance.

Heer and Waffen-SS platoons in a 150. Panzerbrigade Kampfgruppe company ignore the Reich Divided rule (see page 242 of the rulebook) and do not treat each other as Allies.

Enemy Disguises

Skorzeny's troops used captured trucks and painted all of their vehicles green with white stars. The disguises weren't perfect, but they took whatever advantage they could.

A platoon equipped with Enemy Disguises must be Identified before the enemy can shoot at it or assault it. These units start the game unidentified.

If a platoon equipped with Enemy Disguises shoots, conducts anti-aircraft fire, or launches an assault, they are immediately Identified by all enemy platoons.

In order to Identify a platoon equipped with Enemy Disguises, an enemy platoon must attempt to shoot at it or select it as the target for an Artillery Bombardment. Before rolling To Hit or Range In, the platoon rolls a Skill Test.

- If they pass the Skill Test, they Identify the German platoon and shoot at or bombard it as normal. The German unit is now Identified to all enemy platoons.

- If they fail, they do not Identify the unit, but may shoot at or bombard other German platoons instead.

Enemy Recce teams that attempt to shoot at or bombard a platoon equipped with Enemy Disguises automatically Identify them if they are within 8"/20cm.

An AOP or Bunker cannot Identify a platoon equipped with Enemy Disguises. Aircraft cannot choose a team that has not been Identified as the target of an air strike.

FIELDING SKORZENY COMMANDO GROUPS

The role of Skorzeny's commandos is the sew the seeds of panic and confusion amongst the ranks of the American defenders during the opening stages of the Ardennes offensive. This would allow the hard-hitting panzers to then smash through the line of the disorganised enemy.

MOTIVATION AND SKILL

RELUCTANT	CONSCRIPT
CONFIDENT	TRAINED
FEARLESS	**VETERAN**

Skorzeny Commando teams are rated **Fearless Veteran**.

SKORZENY COMMANDO GROUP

2 Skorzeny Commando teams	100 points
1 Skorzeny Commando team	50 points

LIEUTENANT

LIEUTENANT

Skorzany Commando team   Skorzany Commando team

COMMANDO SECTION

SKORZANY COMMANDO GROUP

SPREAD RUMOURS

SKORZENY COMMANDO GROUPS IN FLAMES OF WAR

ATTRIBUTES
Skorzeny Commando teams are unarmed Independent Jeep teams. Being composed entirely of Independent teams, a Skorzeny Commando Group is not a platoon for any purpose whatsoever.

PERFECT DISGUISES
Skorzeny Commando teams are considered friendly teams by your opponent's force, although they do not consider the opponent's teams to be friendly teams. As such, they can never be shot at, used as the Aiming Point for an Artillery Bombardment, or assaulted, by enemy teams. Nor can Skorzeny Commando teams shoot, launch an assault, or perform a Stormtroopers move. However, unlike normal friendly teams, enemy teams can shoot through Skorzeny Commando teams.

Ignore Skorzeny Commando teams completely during artillery bombardments or air attacks, and when determining the Safety Distance for aircraft.

DEPLOYMENT
Skorzeny Commando teams are deployed in your opponent's Deployment Area, immediately after your opponent's Independent Teams have been deployed.

MOVEMENT
Skorzeny Commando teams may only move during your opponent's Movement Step after all of your opponent's teams have moved. Skorzeny Commando teams can move within 2"/5cm of enemy teams, but can never move At the Double.

TIME TO HEAD BACK
If a Skorzeny Commando team ends its Movement Step within 16"/40cm of a friendly team (other than another Skorzeny Commando team) it is removed from play.

EXPOSED
If a Skorzeny Commando team is Exposed (either by being Challenged or by failing in an attempt to Sow Chaos), it is Destroyed and immediately removed from play. This is the only way a Skorzeny Commando team can be Destroyed.

CHALLENGE
During your opponent's Shooting Step, your opponent may Challenge a Skorzeny Commando team with any of their Command teams within 6"/15cm. Instead of shooting, each command team that wishes, to immediately Challenges the Skorzeny Commando team (the rest of the platoon may shoot as normal).

Each time it is Challenged, the Skorzeny Commando team must make an immediate Skill Check:

- If successful, the Skorzeny Commando team answers the challenge correctly and is not Exposed.
- If unsuccessful, the Skorzeny Commando team fails to give the correct answer and is Exposed.

SKORZENY COMMANDO GROUPS

REVERSE ROAD SIGNS

SOWING CHAOS BEHIND ENEMY LINES

The activities of *Unternehmen Greif* (Operation Griffin) were legendary, far beyond truth in many cases! For their size, the Skorzeny Commandos sowed a massive amount of chaos in the early days of the Ardennes offensive. Even Patton's troops as far south as the Lorraine were convinced Skorzeny's men were operating in their area!

During your opponent's Starting Step, Skorzeny Commando teams may attempt to sow chaos amongst your opponent's troops. Once each turn, each Skorzeny Commando team may choose one of the following special rules to use.

SPREAD RUMOURS

Perhaps the best result of *Unternehmen Greif* was the sheer impact of the false rumours and contradictory orders spread by the commandos. The most effective rumour spread by Skorzeny's men was that their ultimate mission was to infiltrate as far as Paris to assassinate General Eisenhower, overall commander of Allied forces. The general's staff was so paranoid they locked Eisenhower away making it difficult for him to conduct the war!

At the beginning of your opponent's Starting Step, immediately before the opponent Rallies Pinned Down Platoons, this Skorzeny Commando team may attempt to Spread Rumours. Choose an enemy platoon within 4"/10cm of this Skorzeny Commando team and Roll a Skill Check:

- *If successful, the commandos spread devious rumours amongst the men of the enemy platoon and it becomes Pinned Down.*
- *Otherwise, the rumours raise suspicion and the Skorzeny Commando team is immediately Exposed.*

REVERSE ROAD SIGNS

One easy way to disrupt an enemy counterattack is to switch road signs, or mark off safe roads with white tape to convince the enemy the road is mined.

At the beginning of your opponent's Starting Step, immediately before the opponent roll for Reserves, this Skorzeny Commando team may attempt to Reverse Road Signs. Roll a Skill Check for the Skorzeny Commando team:

- *If successful, your opponent's Reserves may not arrive anywhere within 12"/30cm of this Skorzeny Commando team during this turn.*
- *Otherwise, the Skorzeny Commando team is caught in the act and it is Exposed.*

If a platoon cannot arrive on the table as a result of this special rule, it returns to Reserve instead.

OBSERVE DEFENCES

The commando teams collected information on enemy defences, troop strength, and other details that would be useful for the advancing German Army.

At the beginning of your opponent's Starting Step, immediately before the opponent Reveals Ambushes, this Skorzeny Commando team may Observe Defences. Roll a Skill Check for the Skorzeny Commando team:

- *If successful, your opponent cannot place teams from Ambush within 8"/20cm and Line Of Sight of this Skorzeny Commando team.*
- *Otherwise, the Skorzeny Commando team draws too much attention to itself and it is Exposed.*

OBSERVE DEFENCES

21

150. PANZERBRIGADE KAMPFGRUPPE
150TH PANZER BRIGADE BATTLE GROUP
TANK COMPANY

MOTIVATION AND SKILL

Platoons from the Heer (marked) are rated **Confident Veteran.**

Platoons from the Waffen-SS (marked) are rated **Fearless Veteran.**

HEER		WAFFEN-SS	
RELUCTANT	CONSCRIPT	RELUCTANT	CONSCRIPT
CONFIDENT	TRAINED	CONFIDENT	TRAINED
FEARLESS	**VETERAN**	**FEARLESS**	**VETERAN**

HEADQUARTERS

- 150. Panzerbrigade Kampfgruppe HQ — 23

You must field one platoon from each box shaded black and may field one platoon from each box shaded grey.

Your Company HQ is from the Waffen-SS (marked). At least one Combat Platoon must also be from the Waffen-SS, however the remainder of your force can be of any type.

COMBAT PLATOONS

ARMOUR OR INFANTRY
- Ersatz Panther Platoon — 23
- SS-Jäger Platoon — 24
- Fallschirmkommando Platoon — 25

ARMOUR OR INFANTRY
- Ersatz StuG Platoon — 24
- SS-Jäger Platoon — 24
- Fallschirmkommando Platoon — 25

INFANTRY
- SS-Jäger Platoon — 24
- Fallschirmkommando Platoon — 25

SUPPORT PLATOONS

WEAPONS PLATOONS

RECONNAISSANCE
- Skorzeny Commando Group — 20

INFANTRY
- Gepanzerte Panzergrenadier Platoon — 25

ANTI-TANK
- Anti-tank Platoon — 26

ARTILLERY
- Heavy Mortar Platoon — 26

RECONNAISSANCE
- Ersatz Panzerspäh Platoon — 27

RECONNAISSANCE
- Skorzeny Commando Group — 20

INFANTRY
- Pionier Platoon — 27
- Gepanzerte Panzergrenadier Platoon — 25

ANTI-TANK
- Anti-tank Platoon — 26

ARTILLERY
- Heavy Mortar Platoon — 26

AIRCRAFT
- Air Support — 15

Remember, Heer and Waffen-SS platoons in a 150. Panzerbrigade Kampfgruppe company ignore the Reich Divided rule.

HEADQUARTERS

150. PANZERBRIGADE KAMPFGRUPPE HQ

HEADQUARTERS

Company HQ	55 points

OPTIONS
- Replace either or both Command SMG teams with Command Panzerfaust SMG teams for +10 points per team.
- Replace either or both Captured Jeeps with Sd Kfz 250 half-tracks for +10 points per half-track.

HAUPTSTURMFÜHRER
HAUPTSTURMFÜHRER

Company Command SMG team — Captured Jeep — 2iC Command SMG team — Captured Jeep

COMPANY HQ

150. PANZERBRIGADE KAMPFGRUPPE HQ

While any team from a 150. Panzerbrigade Kampfgruppe HQ is mounted in its Captured Jeep Transport team, it uses the Enemy Disguises special rule on page 19.

At the core of each *Kampfgruppe* was the SS troopers from Skorzeny's veteran commandos of *502. SS-Jägerbataillon* (502nd SS-Light Infantry Battalion).

COMBAT PLATOONS

ERSATZ PANTHER PLATOON

PLATOON

5 Ersatz Panther	920 points
4 Ersatz Panther	730 points
3 Ersatz Panther	550 points

An Ersatz Panther Platoon uses the Enemy Disguises special rule on page 19.

The *Ersatz*, or substitute, Panther tanks of *Kampfgruppe X* were done up to look like American M10 tank destroyers by adding thin metal plates on the sides of the turrets and the hull front and rear. The commander's cupola was removed from the turret and outer stowage was removed from the hull.

These tanks offered the grenadiers plenty of firepower and, being Panthers, were generally untouchable from the front.

LEUTNANT
LEUTNANT

Command Ersatz Panther

HQ TANK

UNTEROFFIZIER — **UNTEROFFIZIER**

Ersatz Panther — Ersatz Panther
Ersatz Panther — Ersatz Panther

PANZER SECTION — **PANZER SECTION**

ERSATZ PANTHER PLATOON

Ersatz StuG Platoon

Platoon

5 Ersatz StuG	475	points
4 Ersatz StuG	380	points
3 Ersatz StuG	285	points

An Ersatz StuG Platoon uses the Enemy Disguises special rule on page 19.

No one really knows what the modified StuG assault guns were meant to look like. Most presume that the modified side skirts and raised rear deck tried to emulate the American self-propelled M7 Priest. The assault guns formed the core of *Kampfgruppe Y* and led the assault on Malmédy.

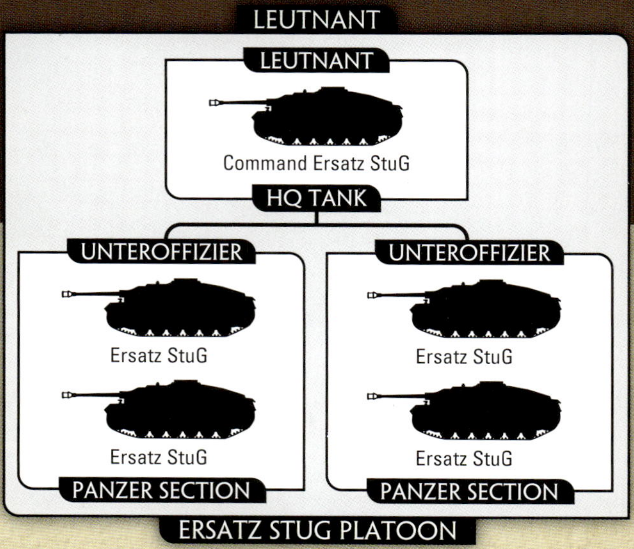

LEUTNANT
Command Ersatz StuG
HQ TANK

UNTEROFFIZIER — Ersatz StuG, Ersatz StuG — **PANZER SECTION**

UNTEROFFIZIER — Ersatz StuG, Ersatz StuG — **PANZER SECTION**

ERSATZ STUG PLATOON

SS-Jäger Platoon

Platoon

HQ Section with:

3 Jäger Squads	190	points

Option
- Replace Command Rifle/MG team with a Command Panzerfaust SMG team for +10 points.

While all Infantry teams in an SS-Jäger Platoon are mounted in their Transport teams, the platoon uses the Enemy Disguises special rule on page 19.

The core infantry of *150. Panzerbrigade* were a wide mix of elite infantry, centred around a company from Skorzeny's own *502. SS-Jägerbataillon* (502nd SS-Light Infantry Battalion).

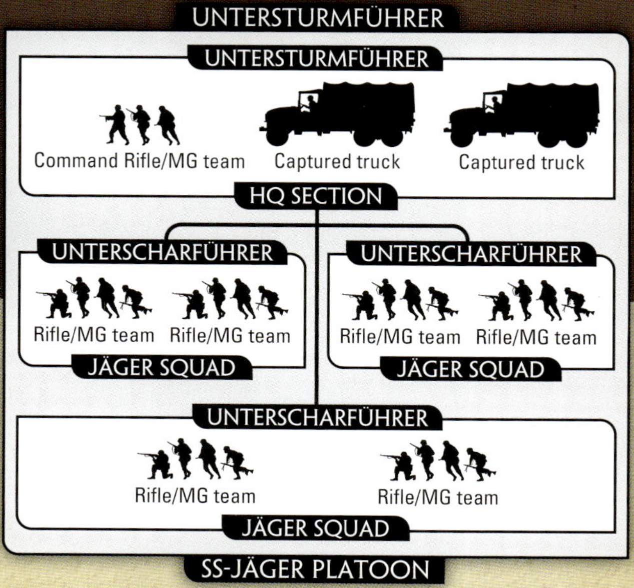

UNTERSTURMFÜHRER
Command Rifle/MG team, Captured truck, Captured truck
HQ SECTION

UNTERSCHARFÜHRER — Rifle/MG team, Rifle/MG team — **JÄGER SQUAD**

UNTERSCHARFÜHRER — Rifle/MG team, Rifle/MG team — **JÄGER SQUAD**

UNTERSCHARFÜHRER — Rifle/MG team, Rifle/MG team — **JÄGER SQUAD**

SS-JÄGER PLATOON

Fallschirmkommando Platoon

PLATOON

HQ Section with:	
3 Fallschirmjäger Squads	265 points
2 Fallschirmjäger Squads	185 points

OPTION
- Replace Command Rifle/MG team with Command Panzerfaust SMG team for +10 points.

The brigade was reinforced by two companies of *600. SS-Fallschirmjäger Abteilung* (600th SS-Paratrooper Battalion), and two battalions of paratroopers from *Sonderverband Jungwirth* (Special Unit Jungwirth), a *Luftwaffe* commando formation.

The *Luftwaffe* personnel were veteran *Fallschirmjäger*, including their commander Hans Jungwirth, who was instrumental in helping cut Hell's Highway during Operation Market Garden. The SS paratroopers have also seen some action and are highly trained and determined soldiers.

LEUTNANT OR OBERFELDWEBEL

LEUTNANT — Command Rifle/MG team
HQ SECTION

OBERJÄGER / OBERJÄGER
Rifle/MG team, Rifle/MG team, Rifle/MG team, Rifle/MG team, Rifle/MG team, Rifle/MG team
FALLSCHIRMJÄGER SQUAD / FALLSCHIRMJÄGER SQUAD

OBERJÄGER
Rifle/MG team, Rifle/MG team, Rifle/MG team
FALLSCHIRMJÄGER SQUAD

FALLSCHIRMKOMMANDO PLATOON

WEAPONS PLATOONS

Gepanzerte Panzergrenadier Platoon

PLATOON

HQ Section with:	
3 Panzergrenadier Squads	220 points
2 Panzergrenadier Squads	155 points

OPTIONS
- Replace the Command MG team with a Command Panzerfaust SMG team for +10 points.
- Replace any or all Sd Kfz 251/1 half-tracks with Sd Kfz 250 half-tracks or Captured M3 half-tracks at no cost.

Gepanzerte Panzergrenadier Platoons may use the Mounted Assault special rule (see page 243 of the rulebook).

While all Infantry teams in a Gepanzerte Panzergrenadier Platoon are mounted in Captured M3 half-tracks, the platoon uses the Enemy Disguises special rule on page 19.

LEUTNANT OR OBERFELDWEBEL

Command MG team — Sd Kfz 251/1 half-track
HQ SECTION

UNTEROFFIZIER / UNTEROFFIZIER
MG team, MG team, MG team, MG team
Sd Kfz 251/1 half-track / Sd Kfz 251/1 half-track
PANZERGRENADIER SQUAD / PANZERGRENADIER SQUAD

UNTEROFFIZIER
MG team, MG team, Sd Kfz 251/1 half-track
PANZERGRENADIER SQUAD

GEPANZERTE PANZERGRENADIER PLATOON

The *Heer* (Army) lent support in the form of a company of *Gepanzerte* (Armoured) Panzergrenadiers, which were used as a reserve shock force.

150. PANZERBRIGADE KAMPFGRUPPE

Anti-tank Gun Platoon

Platoon

HQ Section with:

4 7.5cm PaK40	205 points
3 7.5cm PaK40	155 points
2 7.5cm PaK40	105 points

Option
- Add 3-ton trucks to the platoon for +5 points for the platoon.

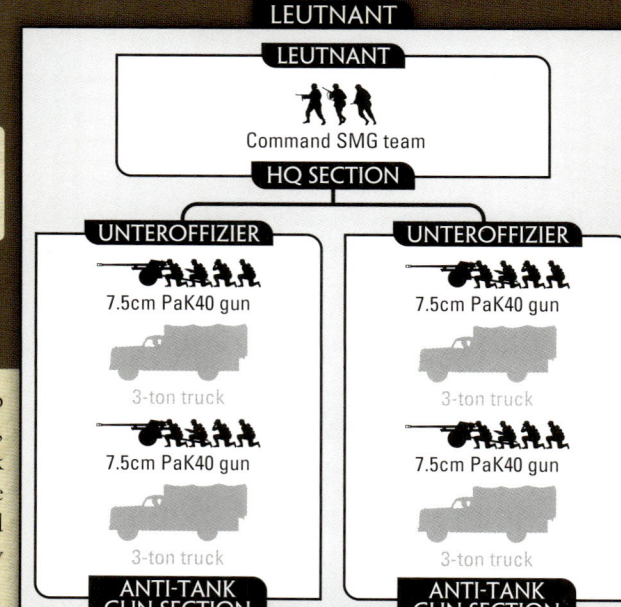

Skorzeny's anti-tank gunners supported the battlegroup with the reliable 7.5cm PaK40 anti-tank gun. Originally, the brigade was to receive American M1 57mm anti-tank guns. They arrived in time for the offensive, but all of the captured ammunition for these guns accidentally detonated while being unloaded off the supply train. Skorzeny quickly abandoned them for the far superior PaK40 instead.

LEUTNANT
- LEUTNANT
- Command SMG team
- HQ SECTION

UNTEROFFIZIER
- 7.5cm PaK40 gun
- 3-ton truck
- 7.5cm PaK40 gun
- 3-ton truck
- ANTI-TANK GUN SECTION

UNTEROFFIZIER
- 7.5cm PaK40 gun
- 3-ton truck
- 7.5cm PaK40 gun
- 3-ton truck
- ANTI-TANK GUN SECTION

ANTI-TANK GUN PLATOON

Heavy Mortar Platoon

Platoon

HQ Section with:

4 12cm sGW43	160 points
2 12cm sGW43	80 points

Option
- Add Kübelwagen jeep and 3-ton trucks for +5 points for the platoon.

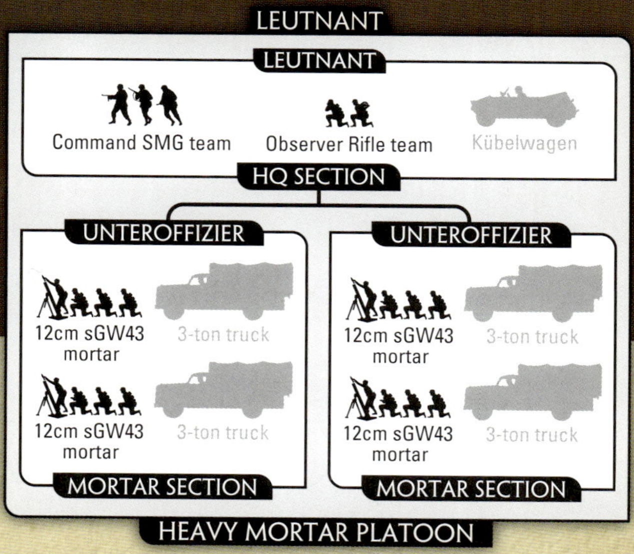

Each of the three battlegroups had a pair of heavy mortar platoons. These weapons were given to the brigade by the Führer Grenadier Brigade and crewed by expert gunners of I. Bataillon, 40. Artillerieregiment (1st Battalion, 40th Artillery Regiment). These heavy mortars were ideal for the highly mobile brigade and provided quick and accurate artillery support.

LEUTNANT
- LEUTNANT
- Command SMG team
- Observer Rifle team
- Kübelwagen
- HQ SECTION

UNTEROFFIZIER
- 12cm sGW43 mortar
- 3-ton truck
- 12cm sGW43 mortar
- 3-ton truck
- MORTAR SECTION

UNTEROFFIZIER
- 12cm sGW43 mortar
- 3-ton truck
- 12cm sGW43 mortar
- 3-ton truck
- MORTAR SECTION

HEAVY MORTAR PLATOON

BRIGADE SUPPORT PLATOONS

Ersatz Panzerspäh Platoon

Platoon

3 Captured M8 Greyhound	135 points
3 Sd Kfz 234/2 Puma	150 points
3 Sd Kfz 234/3 (7.5cm)	140 points

LEUTNANT
- Command Armored car
- Armored car
- Armored car

PANZERSPÄH PATROL

ERSATZ PANZERSPÄH PLATOON

An Ersatz Panzerspäh Platoon equipped with Captured M8 Greyhound uses the Enemy Disguises special rule on page 19.

An Ersatz Panzerspäh Platoon equipped with Captured M8 Greyhound or Sd Kfz 234/2 Puma teams is a Reconnaissance Platoon.

Skorzeny was given ten Allied armoured cars. However only four of them were American and the rest were British. The British ones quickly broke down during training, leaving the captured M8s to do the work. To help bolster the numbers, Skorzeny also acquired three Sd Kfz 234/2 Puma and three Sd Kfz 234/3 (7.5cm) armoured cars. The veteran recon crews came from *2. Panzerdivision* and *90. Panzergrenadierdivision*.

Pionier Platoon

Platoon

HQ Section with:

3 Pioneer Squads	235 points
2 Pioneer Squads	165 points

Options
- Replace Command Pioneer Rifle team with Command Pioneer Panzerfaust SMG team for +10 points.
- Add Pioneer Supply truck for +25 points.

You may replace up to one Pioneer Rifle team per Pioneer Squad with a Flame-thrower team at the start of the game before deployment.

Pioneers were provided to make sure that the way was clear for the brigade, but also to help disarm American demolition charges and quickly throw up assault bridges.

LEUTNANT
- Command Pioneer Rifle team
- Pioneer Supply truck

HQ SECTION

UNTEROFFIZIER
- Pioneer Rifle team
- Pioneer Rifle team
- Pioneer Rifle team

PIONEER SQUAD

UNTEROFFIZIER
- Pioneer Rifle team
- Pioneer Rifle team
- Pioneer Rifle team

PIONEER SQUAD

UNTEROFFIZIER
- Pioneer Rifle team
- Pioneer Rifle team
- Pioneer Rifle team

PIONEER SQUAD

PIONIER PLATOON

150. PANZERBRIGADE KAMPFGRUPPE

GERMAN ARSENAL

TANK TEAMS

Name *Weapon*	Mobility *Range*	Front *ROF*	Armour Side *Anti-tank*	Top *Firepower*	Equipment and Notes
TANKS					
Panzer IV J	Standard Tank	6	3	1	Co-ax MG, Hull MG, Protected ammo, Schürzen.
7.5cm KwK40 gun	*32"/80cm*	*2*	*11*	*3+*	*Slow traverse.*
Panther G	Standard Tank	10	5	1	Co-ax MG, Hull MG, Wide tracks.
7.5cm KwK42 gun	*32"/80cm*	*2*	*14*	*3+*	
Königstiger (Henschel)	Slow Tank	15	8	2	Co-ax MG, Hull MG, Overloaded.
8.8cm KwK43 gun	*40"/100cm*	*2*	*16*	*3+*	*Slow traverse.*
ERSATZ TANKS					
Ersatz StuG G	Standard Tank	7	3	1	Hull MG, Enemy disguises, Protected ammo, Schürzen.
7.5cm StuK40 gun	*32"/80cm*	*2*	*11*	*3+*	*Hull mounted.*
Ersatz Panther	Standard Tank	10	5	1	Co-ax MG, Hull MG, Enemy disguises, Limited vision, Wide tracks.
7.5cm KwK42 gun	*32"/80cm*	*2*	*14*	*3+*	
INFANTRY SUPPORT					
Sd Kfz 251/2 D (8cm)	Half-tracked	1	0	0	AA MG.
8cm GW34 mortar	*24"/60cm*	*2*	*2*	*3+*	*Hull mounted, Portee, Smoke, Minimum range 8"/20cm.*
Firing bombardments	*40"/100cm*	*-*	*2*	*6*	*Smoke bombardment.*
Sd Kfz 251/9 D (7.5cm)	Half-tracked	1	0	0	AA MG.
7.5cm KwK37 gun	*24"/60cm*	*2*	*9*	*3+*	*Hull mounted.*
Sd Kfz 251/17 D (2cm)	Half-tracked	1	0	0	Carry 1 Passenger, Passenger-fired AA MG.
2cm FlaK38 gun	*16"/40cm*	*4*	*5*	*5+*	*Anti-aircraft.*
Sd Kfz 251/1 D (Stuka) half-track	Half-tracked	1	0	0	Hull MG.
28cm sW40 rocket launcher	*40"/100cm*	*-*	*3*	*1+*	*Hull mounted, Stuka zu Fuss.*
Grille (15cm sIG) K	Standard Tank	0	0	0	AA MG.
15cm sIG33 gun	*16"/40cm*	*1*	*13*	*1+*	*Hull mounted, Bunker buster.*
Firing bombardments	*56"/140cm*	*-*	*4*	*2+*	
ANTI-AIRCRAFT (SELF-PROPELLED)					
Sd Kfz 10/5 (2cm)	Half-tracked	-	-	-	Gun shield.
2cm FlaK38 gun	*16"/40cm*	*4*	*5*	*5+*	*Anti-aircraft.*
Sd Kfz 7/1 (Quad 2cm)	Half-tracked	-	-	-	Gun shield.
2cm FlaK38 (V) gun	*16"/40cm*	*6*	*5*	*5+*	*Anti-aircraft.*
Sd Kfz 7/2 (3.7cm)	Half-tracked	-	-	-	Gun shield.
3.7cm FlaK43 gun	*24"/60cm*	*4*	*6*	*4+*	*Anti-aircraft.*
Wirbelwind (Quad 2cm)	Standard Tank	3	1	0	Hull MG.
2cm FlaK38 (V) gun	*16"/40cm*	*6*	*5*	*5+*	*Anti-aircraft.*
Möbelwagen (3.7cm)	Standard Tank	0	0	0	
3.7cm FlaK43 gun	*24"/60cm*	*4*	*6*	*4+*	*Anti-aircraft.*
Ostwind (3.7cm)	Standard Tank	3	1	0	Hull MG.
3.7cm FlaK43 gun	*24"/60cm*	*4*	*6*	*4+*	*Anti-aircraft.*
RECONNAISSANCE					
Captured M8 Greyhound	Wheeled	1	0	0	Co-ax MG, .50 cal AA MG, Enemy disguises, Recce.
M6 37mm gun	*24"/60cm*	*2*	*7*	*4+*	
Sd Kfz 234/1 (2cm)	Jeep	3	0	0	Co-ax MG, Recce.
2cm KwK38 gun	*16"/40cm*	*3*	*5*	*5+*	
Sd Kfz 234/2 Puma	Jeep	3	0	0	Co-ax MG, Recce.
5cm KwK39 gun	*24"/60cm*	*2*	*9*	*4+*	
ARMOURED CAR SUPPORT					
Sd Kfz 234/3 (7.5cm)	Jeep	3	0	0	Hull MG.
7.5cm KwK37 gun	*24"/60cm*	*2*	*9*	*3+*	*Hull mounted.*

GERMAN ARSENAL

Name	Mobility	Front	Armour Side	Top	Equipment and Notes
Weapon	*Range*	*ROF*	*Anti-tank*	*Firepower*	

VEHICLE MACHINE-GUNS

Vehicle MG	*16"/40cm*	*3*	*2*	*6*	*ROF 1 if other weapons fire.*
.50 cal Vehicle MG	*16"/40cm*	*3*	*4*	*5+*	*ROF 1 if other weapons fire.*

INFANTRY TEAMS

Team	Range	ROF	Anti-tank	Firepower	Notes
Rifle team	16"/40cm	1	2	6	
Rifle/MG team	16"/40cm	2	2	6	
MG team	16"/40cm	3	2	6	ROF 2 when Pinned Down.
SMG team	4"/10cm	3	1	6	Full ROF when moving.
Flame-thrower team	4"/10cm	2	-	6	Flame-thrower.
Staff team	16"/40cm	1	2	6	Automatic rifles, Moves as a Heavy Gun team.

ADDITIONAL TRAINING AND EQUIPMENT

Panzerfaust	4"/10cm	1	12	5+	Tank Assault 6, Cannot shoot in the Shooting Step if moved in the Movement Step.

Pioneer teams are rated as Tank Assault 4.

GUN TEAMS

Weapon	Mobility	Range	ROF	Anti-tank	Firepower	Notes
MG42 HMG	Man-packed	24"/60cm	6	2	6	ROF 3 when pinned down or moving.
8cm GW34 mortar	Man-packed	24"/60cm	2	2	3+	Smoke, Minimum range 8"/20cm.
Firing bombardments		40"/100cm	-	2	6	Smoke bombardment.
12cm sGW43 mortar	Light	56"/140cm	-	3	3+	
7.5cm PaK40 gun	Medium	32"/80cm	2	12	3+	Gun shield.
10.5cm leFH18/40 howitzer	Heavy	24"/60cm	1	10	2+	Breakthrough gun, Gun shield, Smoke.
Firing bombardments		72"/180cm	-	4	4+	Smoke bombardment.
15cm sFH18 howitzer	Immobile	24"/60cm	1	13	1+	Bunker buster, Smoke.
Firing bombardments		80"/200cm	-	5	2+	Smoke bombardment.

TRANSPORT TEAMS

Vehicle	Mobility	Front	Armour Side	Top	Equipment and Notes
Weapon	*Range*	*ROF*	*Anti-tank*	*Firepower*	

TRUCKS

Kfz 15 field car or Kübelwagen jeep	Jeep	-	-	-	
Captured jeep	Jeep	-	-	-	Enemy disguises.
Opel Blitz 3-ton truck, or Kfz 68 radio truck	Wheeled	-	-	-	
Captured truck	Wheeled	-	-	-	Enemy disguises.
Opel Maultier	Half-tracked	-	-	-	
Sd Kfz 7 half-track	Half-tracked	-	-	-	

ARMOURED TRANSPORTS

Sd Kfz 250 half-track	Half-tracked	1	0	0	Hull MG. Passenger-fired AA MG.
Sd Kfz 251/1 D half-track	Half-tracked	1	0	0	Hull MG. Passenger-fired AA MG.
Sd Kfz 251/7 D (Pioneer) half-track	Half-tracked	1	0	0	Hull MG. Passenger-fired AA MG, Assault bridge.
M3 half-track	Half-tracked	1	0	0	AA MG. Enemy disguises.

AIRCRAFT

Aircraft	Weapon	To Hit	Anti-tank	Firepower	Notes
Me 262 A2a Sturmvogel	Cannon	3+	9	5+	High-speed Jet.
	Bombs	4+	5	2+	

PAINTING GERMANS
PANZERBRIGADE 150

BASE COLOUR

The MAN factory, where the vehicles for *150. Panzerbrigade* were disguised, was supposed to paint them Olive Drab. There is no way of knowing now whether they had a captured supply of US Olive Drab paint, or whether they had to improvise with whatever they had available. If you wish, you can paint your vehicles Olive Drab, following the US painting guide opposite.

For Battlefront's studio army, we painted our disguised vehicles German *Olivgrün* (Olive Green), using **Reflective Green (890)**, as we guessed that this was most likely the closest paint available.

MUZZLE BRAKES

Photographs show that some of the disguised vehicles had the muzzle brakes removed from their guns. Both options are included, so you can use whichever you prefer.

MARKINGS

Markings on the disguised vehicles are fairly simple: plenty of white stars. The **US Decal Set (US941)** is perfect for this. The disguised StuG assault guns had plain stars, while the Ersatz M10 tank destroyers mostly had stars within circles. Photographs show that at least one M10 had interesting turret markings, with the white circle painted over. This effect is easy to achieve by painting over the decal.

The commando units of Operation *Greif* wore US uniform, so you should follow the painting guide on the opposite page. The only visible difference is the pink or blue scarves they were supposed to wear, to allow them to recognise one another.

PAINTING AMERICANS

AMERICAN INFANTRY

PAINTING GUIDES

- **Green Grey (886)** — Webbing
- **Brown Violet (887)** — Helmet
- **Red Leather (818)** — Helmet Strap, Rifle Sling
- **Flat Flesh (955)** — Exposed skin
- **Gunmetal Grey (863)** — Gun metal
- **Beige Brown (875)** — Rifle wood
- **Khaki (988) or US Dark Green (893)** — Jacket
- **US Field Drab (873)** — Greatcoat
- **US Field Drab (873) or US Dark Green (893)** — Trousers
- **Black (950) or Red Leather (818)** — Boots

All colour names and codes given are for the Vallejo range of Flames Of War paints, available from the online store and Flames Of War stockists. More comprehensive painting and modelling guides can also be found on the www.FlamesOfWar.com website.

AMERICAN VEHICLES

OLIVE DRAB

The painting of US equipment was nothing if not consistent. Almost every tank, truck, gun and was painted the same Olive Drab. Mix a little **Khaki (988)** with **Brown Violet (887)** to add highlights and weathering. The more Khaki you add, the dustier and more faded the vehicle will look. The **US Decal Set (US941)** has markings suitable for most vehicles. For guidance on where to place markings, do an Internet image search.

- **Brown Violet (887) or US Armour Mid/Late (SP03)** — Vehicles, guns, equipment
- Tank name
- Serial Number
- Six stars of various sizes and shapes.

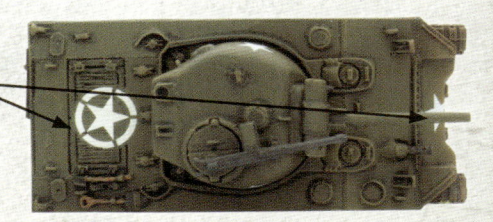

100%

HOLDING THE LINE

14th Cavalry Group M8 armored cars and supporting M8 Scott asssult guns counterattack a *Fallschirmjäger* Platoon.

The 'Damn Engineers' of US 291st battalion prepare to destroy a bridge before a *Königstiger* heavy tank can cross.

US Riflemen man their defences as the they are hit by another German Panther tank-led assault.

Towed and self-propelled tank destroyers lurk ready to pounce on approaching German tanks and infantry.

Forced to stay on the roads by soft ground, a German panzer column falls prey to ambushing Americans.

THE BLOODY BUCKET
THE 28TH INFANTRY DIVISION

The 28th Infantry Division was formed in 1941 from units of the Pennsylvania Army National Guard. Pennsylvania's moniker, the 'Keystone state' led to the division's nickname, 'Keystone'. It later gained the nickname 'Bloody Bucket' division by the Germans owing to its red keystone-shaped insignia.

The division reached France in July 1944 and fought at St. Lô. It pursued the Germans across France with heavy fighting along the way, under the leadership of Major General Norman 'Dutch' Cota. The Keystone men reached the Siegfried Line on the German border on 11 September 1944.

The 28th hammered away at the Siegfried Line until November when it moved north to fight in the bloody battles of the Hürtgen Forest. These terrible battles went back and forth, sapping the strength of the division until, finally on the 19 November, the division was pulled out of the line to rest.

OUT OF THE FRYING PAN…

The 28th moved south to recover from the harrowing battles of Hürtgen to a quiet portion of the line along the Our River in the Ardennes. Spa pools and United Service Organizations (USO) entertainment shows, including a visit from the famous Marlene Dietrich, helped ease the men's minds as they took up a large stretch of the line with its three regiments, 109th, 110th, and 112th covering nearly 25 miles (40km) long. Standard doctrine called for an infantry division to cover five miles at most, but since the Allies did not expect any enemy activity in the Ardennes, the sector was chosen as the ideal spot to rest their tired divisions.

…AND INTO THE FIRE

In the pre-dawn hours of 16 December 1944, a German artillery bombardment woke up the Keystone men. In the north, the 116th Panzer Division launched its attack against the 28th's 112th Infantry Regiment, easily overcoming the thinly deployed American outposts. The 112th Regiment bounced back fast, crushing two companies of panzergrenadiers as they attempted to infiltrate at Lützkampen. However, further south *560. Volksgrenadierdivision* cut through the boundary between the 112th and 110th Infantry Regiments, isolating former from the division until January 1945.

ONE REGIMENT VERSUS AN ARMY

The 110th Regiment guarded the division's centre and was by far the hardest hit. Lined up against them were three panzer and two infantry divisions. The Keystone men stubbornly held onto the vital crossings over the Our River, forcing the Germans to commit their precious reserves in order to overrun the Americans. So stout were the American defenders that the Germans had to send battalions to deal with companies or even platoons. Despite the resistance, the

AGAINST THE TIDE

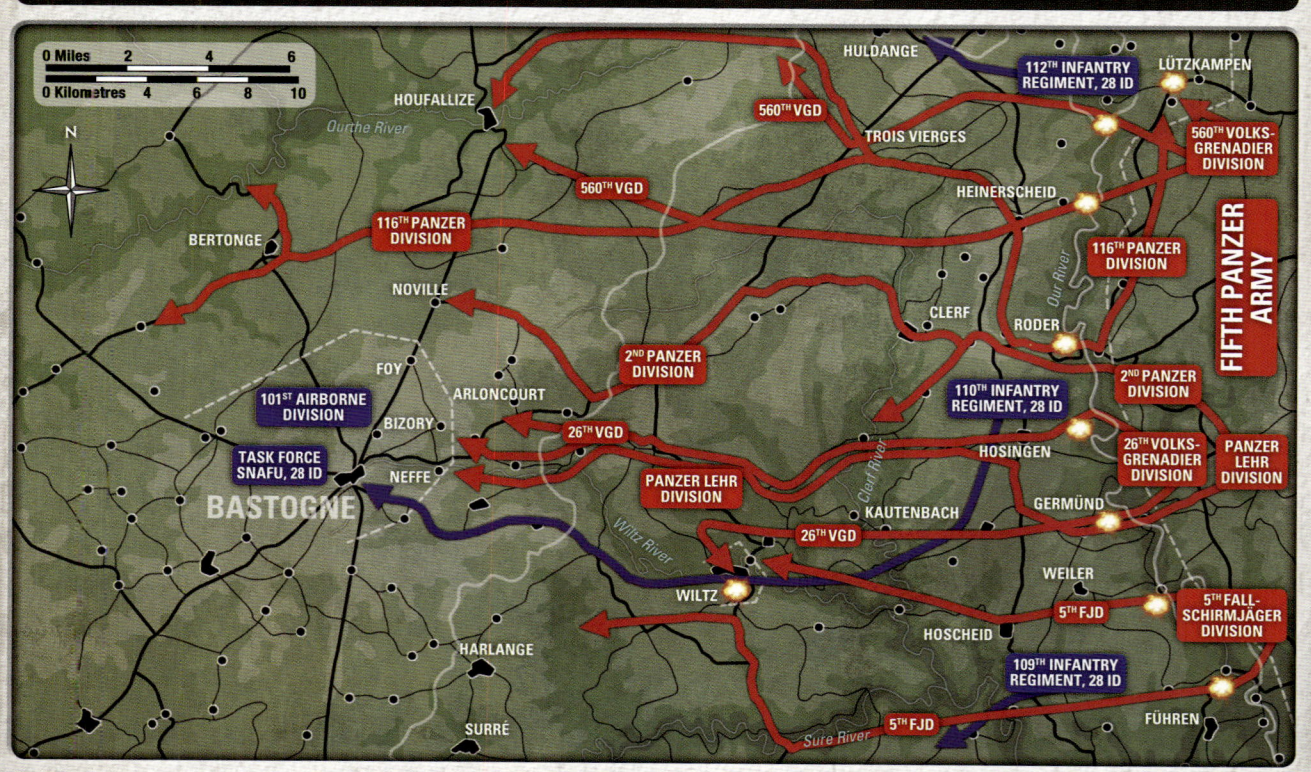

34

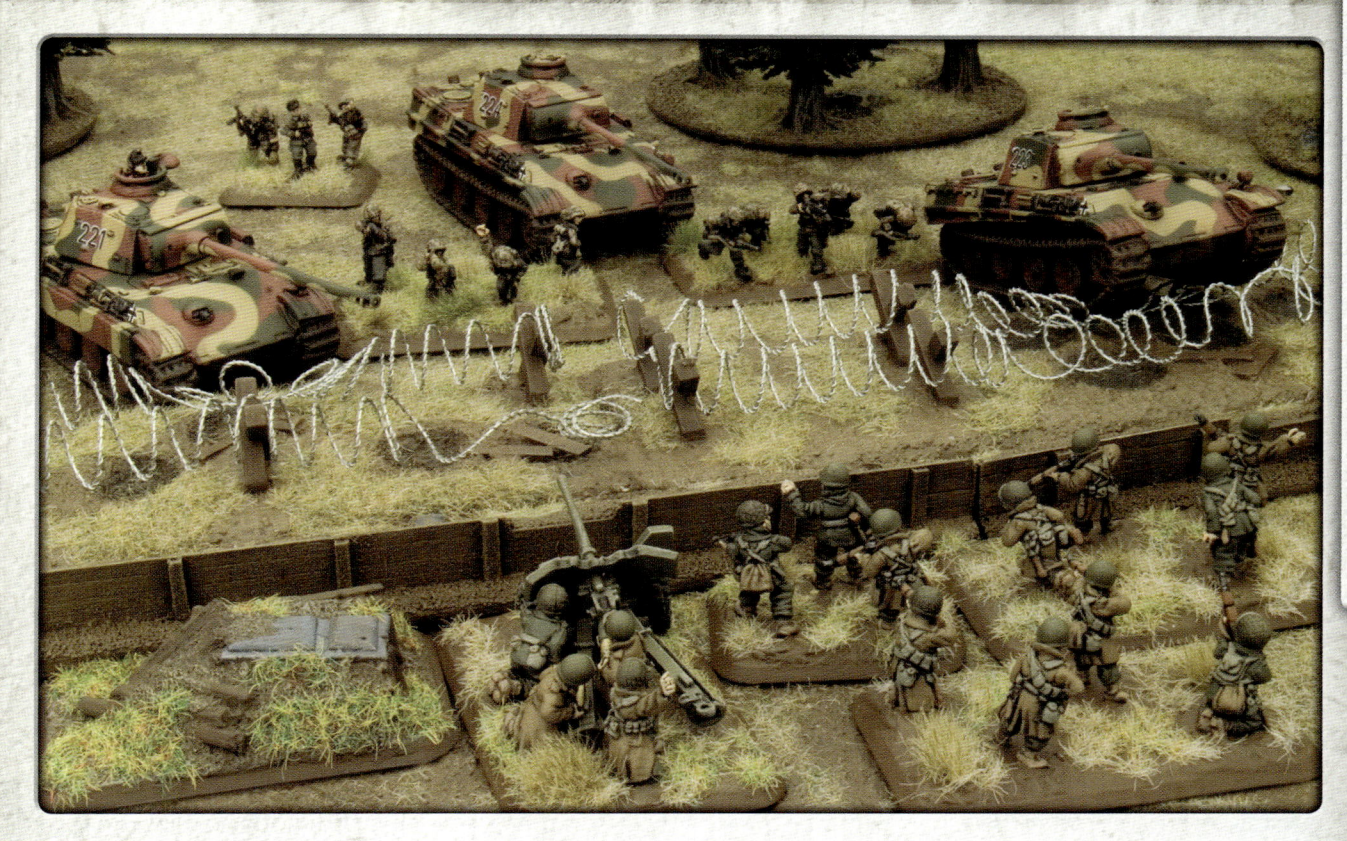

Germans slowly overcame the Americans. The remnants of the 110th infantry made their way back to the Divisional HQ at Wiltz, with the Germans hot on their heels.

The 109th Regiment, commanded by Lieutenant Colonel James Rudder (previously of the 2nd Ranger Battalion at Point-du-Hoc), held the southern flank against the might of the German Seventh Army. The 109th Regiment's companies battled the paratroopers of *5. Fallschirmjägerdivision*. In the early hours of 16 December, the Germans struggled to overcome the American outposts, but did not gain access to the Wiltz road until 18 December, after Rudder's men withdrew south and joined the 4th Infantry Division.

WILTZ

As the 110th Infantry Regiment gave way along the Our River, the Germans were under orders to bypass Wiltz in order to rush Bastogne and capture it as quickly as possible. However, one regiment of the *5. Fallschirmjäger* ignored the order and attacked Wiltz. Soon other German units were sucked into the vortex of battle. The rest of *5. Fallschirmjägerdivision* and following *26. Volksgrenadierdivision* had to be committed to deal with the stubborn Keystone troops of the 110th Infantry Regiment and an ad hoc battalion of staff clerks, cooks, and orderlies. The 110th Infantry Regiment held the German divisions at Wiltz for 24 hours before they were forced to withdraw toward Bastogne. As they withdrew, they made life difficult for the pursuing Germans. In the end the battle had cost the Germans nearly two days urgently need to reach the Meuse before US reinforcements arrived.

The shattered, but not destroyed, 28th Infantry withdrew to the Meuse River and took up positions in the event the Germans made it past Bastogne. Some elements remained in Bastogne, however, forming Task Force SNAFU to help defend the town.

In the wake of *Wacht Am Rhein*, the division was spent. The 110th Infantry Regiment alone was left with less than 600 men from its strength of 3256 on 15 December, and the other regiments were nearly as bad off. Their achievements justified the loses though, as the division held up nine German divisions and bought enough time for the 101st Airborne Division to get to Bastogne ahead of the Germans and deny the enemy the vital crossroads there.

28TH INFANTRY DIVISION SPECIAL RULE

A Rifle Company from the 28th Infantry Division uses all of the normal US special rules found in the rulebook. In addition, they also use the At All Costs special rule.

AT ALL COSTS

With little hope of reinforcements, the thinly deployed line of the 28th Infantry Division was all that stood between the Germans and the vital crossroads of Bastogne. The division bravely fought, buying time for the 101st Airborne Division to arrive.

All platoons of a Perimeter Outposts force start the game in Prepared Positions, even in missions that do not use the Prepared Positions special rule. In addition, all platoons may re-roll failed attempts to Dig In.

PERIMETER OUTPOST
FORTIFIED COMPANY

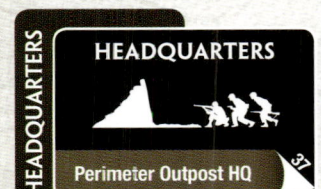

HEADQUARTERS

HEADQUARTERS
Perimeter Outpost HQ — 37

You must field one platoon from each box shaded black and may field one platoon from each box shaded grey.

Your Combat, Weapons, and Regimental support platoons must be from the 28th Infantry Division (marked 🍎).

Support platoons can be of any variant type and do not have to be from the 28th Infantry Division.

COMBAT PLATOONS

INFANTRY
Outpost Platoon — 37

INFANTRY
Outpost Platoon — 37

INFANTRY
Outpost Platoon — 37

INFANTRY
Outpost Platoon — 37

FORTIFICATIONS

FORTIFICATIONS
Outpost Fortifications — 38

WEAPONS PLATOONS

ARTILLERY
Mortar Platoon — 51

INFANTRY
Ammunition & Pioneer Platoon — 52

REGIMENTAL SUPPORT PLATOONS

RECONNAISSANCE
Intelligence & Recon Platoon — 52

ARTILLERY OR ANTI-TANK
Cannon Platoon — 53
Anti-tank Platoon — 51

SUPPORT PLATOONS

ARMOUR OR ANTI-TANK
Tank Platoon — 68
Tank Destroyer Platoon — 69
Towed Tank Destroyer Platoon — 69

ARMOUR
Tank Platoon — 68
Light Tank Platoon — 67

RECONNAISSANCE
Cavalry Recon Platoon — 65

INFANTRY
Engineer Combat Platoon — 59
Parachute Rifle Platoon — 71

ARTILLERY
Field Artillery Battery — 72
Provisional Artillery Battery — 73
Rocket Launcher Battery — 75

ARTILLERY
Calliope Tank Platoon — 54
Chemical Mortar Platoon — 55
Field Artillery Battery — 72
Rocket Launcher Battery — 75

ARTILLERY
Field Artillery Battery — 72
Field Artillery Battery (155mm) — 72
Armored Field Artillery Battery — 74

ANTI-AIRCRAFT
Anti-aircraft Artillery Platoon — 76
Anti-aircraft Artillery (Self-propelled) Platoon — 77

AIRCRAFT
Air Support — 77
Air Observation Post — 77

36

PERIMETER OUTPOST

MOTIVATION AND SKILL

The bloody battles of the Hürtgen Forest sapped the strength of the 28th Infantry Division until, finally on the 19 November, the division was pulled out of the line to rest. However, before the division was fully recovered, they were hit by the German Ardennes offensive. A Perimeter Outpost from the 28th Infantry Division is rated **Reluctant Veteran**.

28TH INFANTRY DIVISION

RELUCTANT	CONSCRIPT
CONFIDENT	TRAINED
FEARLESS	VETERAN

HEADQUARTERS

PERIMETER OUTPOST HQ

HEADQUARTERS

Perimeter Outpost HQ	15 points

OPTIONS
- Replace all Command Carbine teams with Command SMG teams for +10 points per team.
- Add up to three Sniper teams for +50 points per team.

PERIMETER OUTPOST HQ
- FIRST LIEUTENANT: Company Command Carbine team
- FIRST LIEUTENANT: 2iC Command Carbine team
- Trench Line
- COMPANY HQ

COMBAT PLATOONS

OUTPOST PLATOON

PLATOON

HQ Section with:

2 Rifle Squads	115 points
1 Rifle Squad	85 points

OPTIONS
- Replace Command Rifle team with a Command SMG team for +5 points.
- Replace up to one team in each Rifle Squad with a Bazooka team for +5 points per team.
- Add M2 60mm mortar for +20 points.
- Add M1917 HMG for +25 points.
- Add an M1 57mm (late) gun in a Gun Pit for +30 points
- Add up to two Barbed Wire Entanglements for +10 points per entanglement.
- Add up to one Minefield for +50 points.
- Add up to one Anti-tank Obstacle for +100 points.

An Outpost Platoon is a Fortified Platoon (see page 262 of the rulebook).

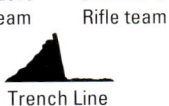

OUTPOST PLATOON

HQ SECTION (SERGEANT): Command Rifle team, Bazooka team, M1919 LMG, Trench Line

RIFLE SQUAD (CORPORAL): Rifle team, Rifle team, Trench Line

RIFLE SQUAD (CORPORAL): Rifle team, Rifle team, Trench Line

WEAPONS SECTION (CORPORAL): M2 60mm mortar, M1917 HMG, M1 57mm (late) gun in Gun Pit

OBSTACLES (FORTIFICATIONS): Barbed Wire Entanglement, Barbed Wire Entanglement, Minefield, Anti-tank Obstacle

37

FORTIFICATIONS

OUTPOST FORTIFICATIONS

FORTIFICATIONS

4 Minefields	200 points
3 Minefields	150 points
2 Minefields	100 points

OPTIONS
- Add up to four Barbed Wire Entanglements for +10 points per entanglement.
- Add up to two Anti-tank Obstacle for +100 points per obstacle.

Outpost Fortifications are Area Defences (see pages 214 and 262 of the rulebook).

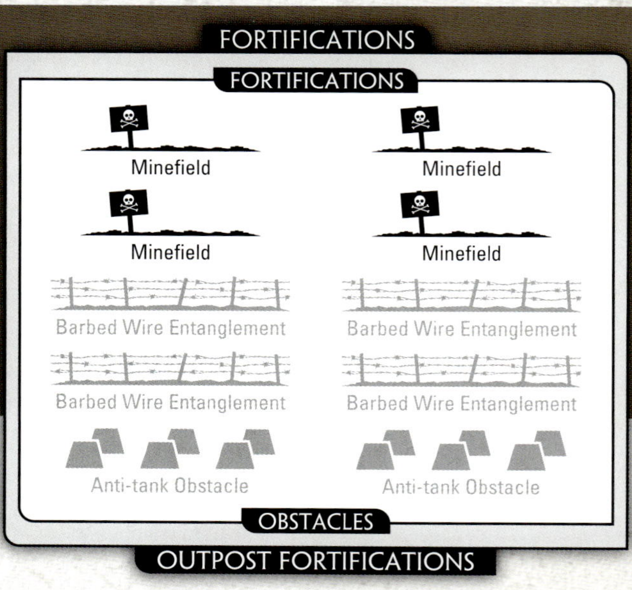

The rifle companies spent early December preparing their winter quarters in the Ardennes. They incorporated the defences of the Siegfried Line into their defensive plan, creating a dense network of mines, barbed wire and obstacles.

FORTIFICATIONS

- Minefield
- Minefield
- Minefield
- Minefield
- Barbed Wire Entanglement
- Barbed Wire Entanglement
- Barbed Wire Entanglement
- Barbed Wire Entanglement
- Anti-tank Obstacle
- Anti-tank Obstacle

OBSTACLES

OUTPOST FORTIFICATIONS

PERIMETER OUTPOST

FIELDING OTHER HÜRTGEN FOREST DIVISIONS

THE 4TH INFANTRY DIVISION

The 'Ivy' (IV being four in Roman numerals) Division was activated in 1940 as the only mechanised division in the US Army. It eventually took on the form of a regular infantry division, but still retained an aggressive and mobile doctrine.

The Ivy Division was the first US division to land in France on D-Day, 6 June 1944, at Utah Beach. It then moved south and relieved the 82nd Airborne Division at Sainte-Mère-Église. After the beachheads were secure, the Ivy division threw its weight into the breakout, working closely with the 2nd Armored Division during Operation Cobra.

After the pursuit across France, the 4th found itself on the German frontier near Bastogne. However, it was soon moved north to fight in the harsh battles of the Hürtgen Forest. After the battle, the exhausted Ivy Division was relocated to the quiet Ardennes south of the 28th's positions to receive reinforcements and a little rest.

When the Ardennes Offensive opened, the 4th was lucky to have a much smaller portion of the line to defend, compared to the 28th's long and thin front. After the first few hours of the battle, the 4th was unintentionally reinforced by the 28th's cut-off 109th Infantry Regiment. They put up a stern defence and the Germans made only small gains. The Ivy Division's steadfast defence formed the core of the southern shoulder of the 'Bulge'.

To field a Perimeter Outpost force from the 4th Infantry Division or another Hürtgen infantry division, simply build your force using the 28th Infantry Division symbol (marked 🛡), ratings, and special rule.

39

INDIANHEADS
THE 2ND INFANTRY DIVISION

The 2nd Infantry Division was formed in September 1917 during World War I. During that war the division's symbol came from a truck driver who had painted it on his truck. His symbol was adopted by the division and soon they became known as the 'Indianheads'.

NORMANDY TO THE GERMAN BORDER

The division, under the command of Major General Walter Robertson, landed on Omaha Beach on D+1 (7 June) 1944 and immediately went to work securing the beach and mopping up German resistance. They then moved inland and fought their way from Saint-Lô to Brittany. The tough fighting in Brittany left the 2nd Infantry an extremely well-organised and highly professional unit.

After Brittany, the division joined the US Army's pursuit of the Germans across France and found itself on the German frontier by December 1944, occupying the region south of Losheim. On 11 December the 2nd Infantry launched an attack with the 78th Infantry Division to capture the dams on the Roer River. The division gave up its position on the line to the newly-arrived 106th Infantry Division and formed up behind the 99th Infantry Division to launch its assault.

Using two of the division's three regiments, the Indianheads attacked on a narrow frontage to smash its way through the Siegfried Line. The 9th and 38th Infantry Regiments had penetrated about seven miles into the German lines when news reached Robertson that the Germans had launched a major offensive on his exposed southern flank. Naïve orders arrived from V Corps to keep moving east, but the experienced Robertson prepared a clever, although complicated plan, to withdraw of his division to safety.

SKINNING THE CAT

On the morning of 17 December, V Corps finally ordered Robertson to withdraw. He quickly put his complicated action plan, nicknamed "Skinning the Cat", into motion. The first of the two attacking regiments had to carefully pull back through the rear battalion of the second regiment. Once that was done they set up defensive positions to allow the other regiment to pass through and so on until they both reached the twin villages of Krinkelt and Rocherath held by the 99th Infantry. Once in the villages, the 99th would then pass through them to the safety of the Elsenborn Ridge, which dominated the area and offered an excellent defensive position for the US troops. The manoeuvre was fraught with peril, as any error in this complex plan would turn the withdrawal into a full rout, but the experienced Indianheads executed it with perfection, reaching Krinkelt by midday.

TWIN VILLAGES

While the 9th and 38th Regiments pulled back, the first of the German attacks struck near Rocherath on 16 December. The Indianheads' third regiment, the 23rd, rushed forward to bolster the line behind the 99th Infantry Division. Just as they reached Rocherath, the Germans struck with *277. Volksgrenadierdivision*, but the infantrymen stood fast with the help of the 612th and 644th Tank Destroyer Battalions as well as the 2nd Infantry's own 741st Tank Battalion.

Frustrated, the Germans committed *12. SS-Panzerdivision* from their reserves. Under the weight of the renewed attack, the 23rd Regiment and the 99th Division were forced to withdraw, but they had bought enough time for the other Indianhead regiments to reach Rocherath and set up behind them.

During the night of 17 December, the 2nd held the line as the 99th retreated to the Elsenborn Ridge, but some of their

BATTLE OF THE TWIN VILLAGES

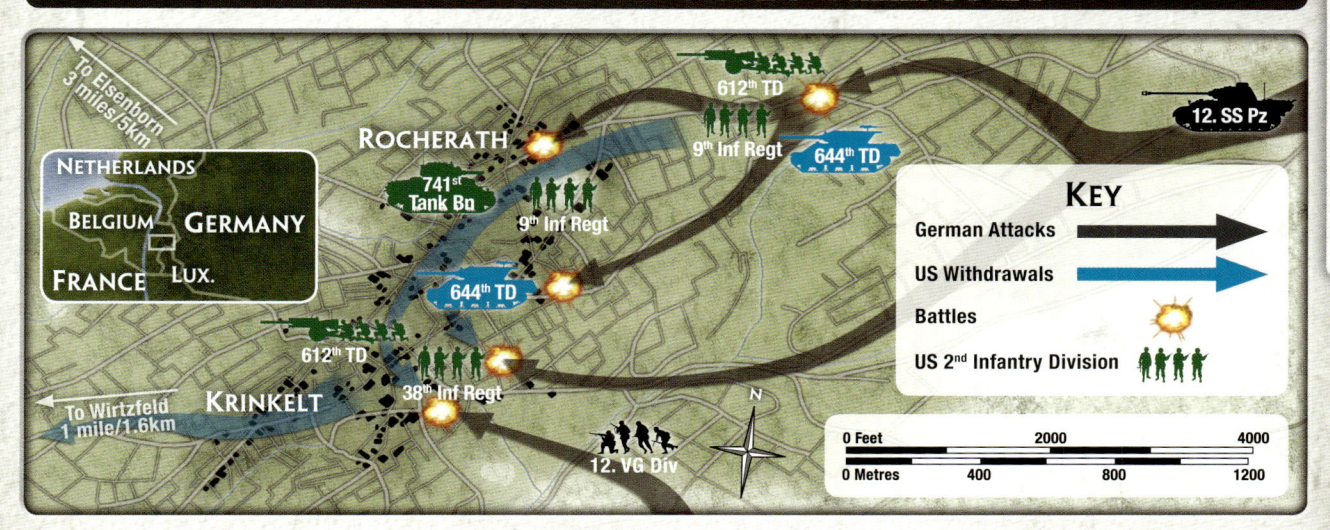

Map Key:
- German Attacks
- US Withdrawals
- Battles
- US 2nd Infantry Division

troops stayed behind and fought alongside the Indianheads in the twin villages. The situation was chaotic—one 2nd Infantry colonel had elements of 16 different companies under his command! Nonetheless the 2nd executed an exemplary defence and by nightfall on 18 December, the 99th had successfully passed through and set up behind the Indianheads. The 2nd Infantry then successfully pulled back to the Elsenborn Ridge.

ELSENBORN RIDGE

The V Corps artillery on the ridge reinforced the two divisions, while the veteran 1st and 9th Infantry Divisions secured their flanks. The Indianheads and the 99th easily repelled three attempts to take the ridge before the Germans gave up.

The tough defenders of the twin villages and the Elsenborn Ridge dealt a fatal blow to *Wacht Am Rhein*, throwing the German timetable hopelessly off schedule and denying the important high ground to the German offensive.

FIELDING OTHER VETERAN DIVISIONS

THE 1ST INFANTRY DIVISION

The 'Big Red One' 1st Infantry Division has seen more than its fair share of the war. Since landing in North Africa in 1943, the division has been involved in nearly every major operation conducted by the US Army.

Before the Ardennes, the Big Red One was resting from pushing its way through the bloody streets of Aachen, the first German town to fall to the Allies. While many divisions came out of that fight a bit worse for wear, the 1st never lost its professionalism, and without hesitation sprang into action to stem the German tide in the Ardennes.

THE 30TH INFANTRY DIVISION

The 30th Infantry Division, known as "Old Hickory" in honour of President Andrew Jackson, arrived in France in June 1944, spearheading the breakout at St. Lô.

In December 1944, the 30th joined the 1st to encircle Aachen before rushing south to meet *Wacht Am Rhein*. The division was assigned to help defend Malmédy, a critical crossroads in the path of *SS-Kampfgruppe* Peiper and Otto Skorzeny's *150. Panzerbrigade*. The professional soldiers of Old Hickory were a welcome sight for the 291st Combat Engineer Battalion and permanently turned the tide at Malmédy.

To field a Rifle Company from the 1st or 30th Infantry Divisions, simply build your force using the 2nd Infantry Division symbol (marked), ratings, and special rules.

THE BATTLE BABIES
THE 99TH INFANTRY DIVISION

The 99th Infantry Division was activated in November 1942 and arrived at the front nearly two years later. The 'Checkerboard' division rushed to Belgium to join V Corps on 12 December 1944. Once in the line, the division got the patronizing nickname, 'Battle Babies' by their veteran comrades owing to the fact that they were fresh from the States with absolutely no prior battle experience.

The 99th supported the 2nd Infantry Division's attack against the Roer Dams and guarded their flank at Büllingen from a possible German counterattack. Their commander, Major General Walter Lauer, deployed his regiments along the line with his 395th Infantry Regiment on the left, the 393rd in the centre, and the 394th on the right.

WACHT AM RHEIN

Unbeknownst to the 99th, the Germans were gearing up for their great offensive opposite to them. The Germans didn't rate the 99th highly and believed that they were a second rate division, at best, that wouldn't hold against the might of the offensive. As such the 99th was targeted as the point through which the Germans would send the tanks and men of the *Waffen-SS* through to the Meuse.

On 16 December, the 99th was attacked by the 1st SS-Panzer Corps. Like elsewhere on the front line, the German artillery severed lines of communication and caused some degree of confusion, but the Battle Babies stood their ground.

THE 395TH INFANTRY REGIMENT

In the north, the 395th was attacked by *326. Volksgrenadierdivision* through the heavily wooded region of the Monschau Forest. Twice the grenadiers struck the Battle Babies' lines and were easily thrown back to their starting positions, blunting the grenadiers' assault.

BUYING TIME ON THE NORTHERN SHOULDER

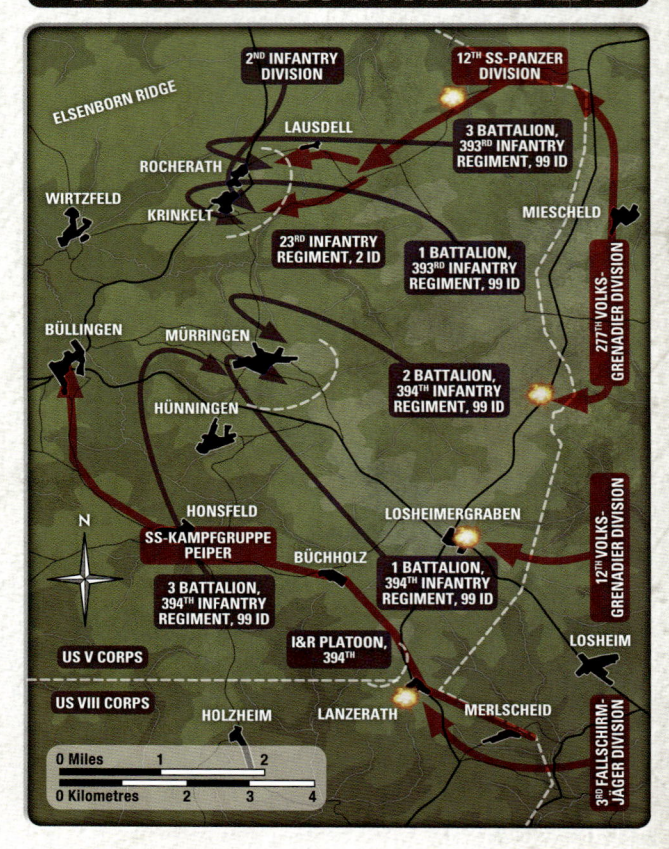

THE TWIN VILLAGES

Further south, the 393rd secured the most important position of the division's line: Krinkelt and Rocherath, also known as the twin villages. This location was critical because it controlled a vital crossroads and high ground, called the Elsenborn Ridge, that the Germans needed to take to secure *SS-Kampfgruppe* Peiper's right flank.

With the 2nd Infantry Division still deep behind enemy lines, Lauer focused on keeping the twin villages open so that the Indianheads could pull back to safety.

277. *Volksgrenadierdivision* attacked through the wooded area east of the twin villages. Bolstered by fortifications left by the Germans as a part of the Siegfried Line, the Checkerboarders held out against the initial onslaught, despite heavy casualties. The frustrated Germans reinforced the attack with a fresh regiment of grenadiers and several Hetzer tank hunters, only to be once more thrown back.

The Germans struck again with a battlegroup of panzergrenadiers and Panzer IV/70 tank hunters from *12. SS-Panzerdivision*. The Americans fought the SS to a standstill; forcing the Germans to commit even more tanks from their precious few reserves to the battle.

The relentless German attack lasted through the night and the Battle Babies withdrew and formed a new line along the Elsenborn Ridge. There the 99th and 2nd Infantry Divisions repulsed several German attempts to storm the ridge.

Defending the Gap

The Losheim Gap, held by the 394th Infantry Regiment, is a clear stretch of ground between the 99th and 106th Infantry Divisions. Several roads and a railroad offered the best going for tanks. With this in mind, it was chosen as *SS-Kampfgruppe* Peiper's main axis of attack.

On 16 December, the 394th Regiment was hit by *3. Fallschirmjägerdivision*. The regiment stalled the German paratroopers at Losheimergraben and Büchholz long enough to buy the Allies time to rush several veteran divisions to the northern shoulder of the bulge.

The Germans greatly underestimated the fighting spirit of the 99th and as a result their plans failed miserably when the Battle Babies fought stubbornly. The defenders had delayed *12. SS-Panzerdivision* for over three days. Not only did they force the Germans to seek a breakthrough elsewhere, they had bought time for reinforcements from the 1st and 30th Infantry, and 82nd Airborne Divisions to arrive.

FIELDING OTHER FRESH DIVISIONS

The 106th Infantry Division

Like the 99th, the 106th Infantry Division was a brand new unit. It was activated in 1943 and reached the front only days before the Ardennes offensive. The 'Golden Lion' Division took over the 2nd Infantry Division's portion of the line when the latter moved north to attack the Roer Dams. Among their responsibilities was to hold St. Vith.

With less than a week to acclimatize itself, the division was torn asunder by the German attack on 16 December 1944. Within hours, the division was cut up into small regimental sections, each completely unable to help the others. One positive note was the fact that the veterans of the 112th Infantry Regiment, 28th Infantry Division, were pushed into their sector and added to their strength.

Tragedy struck when 7000 men from the division's 422nd and 423rd Infantry Regiments were cut off and forced to surrender on 19 December, resulting in the second largest surrender of American forces since the American Civil War. Despite this, the Golden Lions succeeded in delaying the German attack for several days. Several Allied divisions were rushed into the gap to defend St. Vith along with some of the 106th's survivors.

To field a Rifle Company from the 106th Infantry Division or another fresh infantry division, simply build your force using the 99th Infantry Division symbol (marked), ratings, and special rule.

VIKING BATTALION
99TH INFANTRY BATTALION (SEPARATE)

The 99th Infantry Battalion (Separate) was activated in 1942 at Camp Ripley, Minnesota. It was made up entirely of Norwegian-Americans and citizens of Norway who had been trapped in the US after the German invasion of their homeland. In September, the unit moved to Camp Hale, Colorado, where it trained alongside the 10th Mountain Division. The unit's mission was to prepare for a proposed Allied invasion of Norway, but when that did not happen the unit was deployed to France on 30 June 1944.

In August the '99ers' saw its first action in support of the 2nd Armored Division during Operation Cobra. The division's commander praised the 99th for being the only infantry unit his tanks had trouble keeping up with during the war! From there the battalion fought in Holland and then in Germany during the battles around Aachen. By November they were pulled back into the First Army's reserve.

When the Germans attacked through the Ardennes, First Army sent a task force, under the 99th's commanding officer, Major Harold D Hansen, to reinforce the critical town of Malmédy, currently held by elements of the 291st Engineer Combat Battalion. The task force included the 99th, the 526th Armored Infantry Battalion, and the 825th Tank Destroyer Battalion (Towed).

Task Force Hansen made excellent time, despite the horrific traffic jams, and arrived in Malmédy in short order. Hansen deployed his men along a tall railroad embankment overlooking the engineers' roadblock positions. No sooner had the Task Force settled into its positions, than Otto Skorzeny's *150. Panzerbrigade* attacked, reaching the railroad embankment where the 99ers were waiting. The Germans kept trying to take the position, but never shifted the Norwegians.

At the end of the war in Europe on 7 May 1945, the 99th Division was finally sent to Norway to help oversee the surrender of the Germans occupation forces. The 99th returned to the United States and was disbanded on 2 November 1945. It had 101 days in combat, and had received 15 Silver Stars and 20 Bronze Stars to their credit.

FIELDING THE 99TH INFANTRY BATTALION (SEPARATE)

To field a Rifle Company from the 99th Infantry Battalion (Separate), simply build your force using the 2nd Infantry Division Symbol (marked ★). In addition to the normal US special rules found in the rulebook, a Rifle Company from the 99th Infantry Battalion (Separate) uses the following special rules:

SURVIVAL TRAINING

The 99th spent time in the frozen conditions of a Minnesota winter before being moved to a mountain-climbing facility in Colorado to train in 9000-foot (2750m) altitudes.

Infantry and Man-packed Gun teams from the 99th Infantry Battalion (Separate) are Mountaineers (see page 61 of the rulebook). In addition they may move At the Double (using Truscott Trot, see page 239 of the rulebook) through Difficult Going.

SCROUNGE A RIDE

While on garrison duty, the motor company lost no time collecting hundreds of trucks from old worn-out US vehicles to captured German trucks. All of the hard work paid off essentially transforming the battalion into a motorised unit.

When building your force, you must add two Jeep transports to your Rifle Company HQ for +5 points, and two GMC 2½-ton or captured German 3-ton trucks to each of your Rifle platoons for +5 points per platoon.

US SPECIAL RULES

Why We Fight

News of the infamous Malmédy Massacre spread fast, due in no small part to Eisenhower's order to make the incident public. From that moment on, the men gave no quarter to the notorious *Waffen-SS*.

All American platoons from a company with the Why We Fight special rule use the British Bulldog rule (see page 246 of the rulebook) in all Assaults involving any SS platoons.

2ND INFANTRY DIVISION SPECIAL RULE

A Rifle Company from the 2nd Infantry Division uses all of the normal US special rules found on pages 236 to 240 of the rulebook. In addition, they also use the Why We Fight and Winter Training special rules.

Winter Training

The Indianheads received winter training in Sparta, Wisconsin. They trained intensely for four-months during the freezing winter conditions, blizzards, and thick forests of the American upper-Midwest.

Infantry and Man-packed Gun teams from the 2nd Infantry Division may move At the Double (using Truscott Trot, see page 239 of the rulebook) through Difficult Going.

99TH INFANTRY DIVISION SPECIAL RULE

A Rifle Company from the 99th Infantry Division uses all of the normal US special rules found on pages 236 to 240 of the rulebook. In addition, they also use the Why We Fight and Delaying Action special rules.

Delaying Action

The tough defence of the northern shoulder can be attributed in large part to the heroic actions of the "Battle Babies". The 99th fought alongside the Indianheads to bring the German offensive in the north to a standstill.

Company Command teams from the 99th Infantry Division may re-roll the first Company Morale Check that they are required to take if they fail their first attempt.

2ND LIEUTENANT AUDIE MURPHY

"They were killing my friends."

Audie Leon Murphy was born on 20 June 1924 to a farming family in Kingston, Texas. Murphy would go on to be one of America's most famous soldiers and movie stars.

Murphy initially tried to enlist after the attack on Pearl Harbor in 1941, but was turned away because he was underage. Murphy attempted once more on his 18th birthday, but was declined by the Marines, paratroopers, and Navy as too small, being slight man of 5'5½" (166cm) and 110 pounds (50kg). Out of options he joined the infantry.

In early 1943 he was shipped to Morocco as a replacement in 3rd Platoon, Baker Company, I Battalion, 15th Infantry Regiment, 3rd Infantry Division. His combat initiation came when he took part in the invasion of Sicily in July 1943. When the 3rd Division landed at Salerno, Italy, in September 1943 Murphy was in the thick of the fighting earning promotions and decorations for valour.

Murphy's division landed in Southern France in mid-August 1944. During the fighting Murphy's best friend was killed by a German soldier feigning surrender. Murphy, in a fit of vengeful rage, single-handedly wiped out the German machine-gun crew that had just killed his friend. He then went on to destroy several more enemy positions. Murphy received the Distinguished Service Cross for these actions.

In the following seven weeks of fighting, Murphy received two Silver Stars for further heroic actions, and was promoted to staff sergeant. He was later awarded a battlefield commission to 2nd lieutenant, commanding a platoon. He was wounded soon after and spent ten days in hospital. After returning to his unit he became the company commander on 25 January 1945.

The next day, in freezing temperatures and snow, his unit participated in the battle at Holtzwihr on the border between France and Germany. Murphy's battered command consisted just 19 of the company's original 128 men. Murphy ordered his men to take up prepared positions deeper in the wood behind them, while he remained forward to direct artillery fire on the attacking enemy.

Murphy jump aboard a nearby burning M10 tank destroyer, manning its .50 cal machine-gun. With it, he quickly cut down a full squad of German infantry who had crawled down a ditch to within 100 feet (30m) of his position. He received a leg wound, but remained on the tank destroyer firing the .50 cal machine-gun, alternating between calling in artillery and firing bursts from the machine-gun.

Murphy only stopped fighting when his telephone line to the artillery was cut. His remaining men then moved forward and he organized a counter-attack which ultimately drove the enemy from Holtzwihr. For these actions, Murphy was awarded the Medal of Honor, the United States of America's highest military award. After the war he was asked why he had taken on an entire company of German infantry by himself, he replied, 'They were killing my friends'.

Murphy spent the rest of the war as liaison officer. In 27 months in action in the European Theatre Murphy was awarded 33 US and six foreign decorations and medals.

WARRIOR CHARACTERISTICS

You may field 2nd Lieutenant Audie Murphy as either a Company Command Carbine team (replacing the Company Command team in your Rifle Company on page 49) or as a Command Rifle team (replacing the Command Rifle team in one of your Rifle Platoons on page 49) for +35 points. Audie Murphy is a Warrior and is rated **Fearless Veteran**. He does not change the Motivation rating of a platoon he Joins.

THREE PURPLE HEARTS

Murphy received three Purple Hearts during his service, on 15 September 1944, 26 October 1944, and 25 January 1945. The first was for wounds sustained in southern France, the second after he was hit in the hip by a sniper's bullet, and the third when he was wounded by a mortar shell that killed two other men nearby.

If the opponent fails to kill Murphy using the Warrior Infantry Team Casualties rule (see page 106 of the rulebook) you do not need to remove a friendly Infantry team. Murphy, although wounded, fights on alone.

DISTINGUISHED SERVICE CROSS

On 15 August 1944, Murphy earned a Distinguished Service Cross (second highest awards to the Medal of Honor) for his actions during the 3rd Infantry Division's amphibious assault in southern France. When a German machine-gun nest killed one of Murphy's close friends, he flew into a rage and killed every German manning the nest, picked up the machine-gun and a bunch of grenades, and stormed several other German positions nearby.

Murphy may re-roll failed Skill Tests to hit a Bunker in an assault.

TWO BRONZE STARS

Audie Murphy's two Bronze Stars were awarded while he was in Italy. The first was earned during the Anzio landings and the second while the 3rd Infantry Division was attempting to expand the beachhead, when Murphy crawled out into No Man's Land to disable a German tank with rifle grenades.

Audie Murphy has Tank Assault 3.

TWO SILVER STARS

Both of Murphy's Silver Stars were earned in France. The first was awarded on 2 October 1944 after Murphy single-handedly destroyed a machine-gun nest. The second was awarded near Tholy, France on 5 October 1944 when he crawled ahead into No-Man's Land to direct artillery fire on enemy positions.

Murphy may make a Reconnaissance Deployment Move as though he was a Recce team, separately from the rest of his platoon. Note that this might mean that as a Platoon Command team, Murphy begins the game Out of Command.

In addition, as a Command team, Murphy does not incur the usual +1 penalty to the score needed to Range In (see page 126 of the rulebook).

SPECIAL OBJECTIVE CHARACTERISTICS

Instead of fielding 2nd Lieutenant Audie Murphy as a Warrior team, you may field him as a Special Objective in your Rifle Company (page 48), Engineer Combat Company (page 58), Cavalry Reconnaissance Squadron (page 64), or Light Tank Company (page 66) for +25 points.

MEDAL OF HONOR

Audie Murphy single-handedly held off determined German attacks with the .50 cal machine-gun of a burnt-out M10 tank destroyer, despite a leg wound and withering enemy fire. He prevented the Germans from taking his position and the wood that was their ultimate objective with a constant hail of heavy machine-gun fire.

After objectives have been placed, replace any Objective placed in your Deployment Areas with the Audie Murphy Special Objective. If there are no Objectives in your Deployment Area, you cannot use the Special Objective. The Special Objective retains all of the usual rules of an Objective.

In addition, the Audie Murphy Special Objective is also a .50 cal Nest, using the normal Bunker rules found in the rulebook.

The .50 cal Nest can Spot for Artillery Bombardments as if it was a Company Command team, but without the usual +1 penalty to the score needed to Range In (see page 126 of the rulebook). It cannot prevent the enemy from taking Objectives.

If the .50 cal Nest is Destroyed, the Objective reverts to being a normal Objective.

AUDIE MURPHY SPECIAL OBJECTIVE

Weapon	Range	ROF	Anti-tank	Firepower	Notes
.50 cal Nest	16"/40cm	3	4	5+	

RIFLE COMPANY
INFANTRY COMPANY

HEADQUARTERS

Rifle Company HQ — 49

You must field one platoon from each box shaded black and may field one platoon from each box shaded grey.

Your Company HQ must be either from the 2nd Infantry Division (marked ★), or the 99th Infantry Division (marked ▰). All other platoons marked with either of these divisional symbols must be from the same division as your Company HQ.

Support platoons can be of any variant type and do not have to match your Company HQ.

COMBAT PLATOONS

INFANTRY
- Rifle Platoon — 49

INFANTRY
- Rifle Platoon — 49

INFANTRY
- Rifle Platoon — 49

WEAPONS
- Weapons Platoon — 50

SUPPORT PLATOONS

WEAPONS PLATOONS

MACHINE-GUNS
- Machine-gun Platoon — 50

MACHINE-GUNS
- Machine-gun Platoon — 50

ARTILLERY
- Mortar Platoon — 51

ANTI-TANK
- Anti-tank Platoon — 51

INFANTRY
- Ammunition & Pioneer Platoon — 52

REGIMENTAL SUPPORT PLATOONS

ANTI-TANK
- Anti-tank Platoon — 51

RECONNAISSANCE
- Intelligence & Recon Platoon — 52
- Roadblock Strongpoint — 61

ARTILLERY
- Cannon Platoon — 53

ARMOUR

- Scrapyard Tank Platoon — 55
- Tank Platoon — 68
- Tank Destroyer Platoon — 69
- Towed Tank Destroyer Platoon — 69

ARMOUR

- Light Tank Platoon — 67
- Tank Destroyer Platoon — 69
- Towed Tank Destroyer Platoon — 69

INFANTRY

- Rifle Platoon — 49
- Engineer Combat Platoon — 59
- Armored Rifle Platoon — 70
- Roadblock Strongpoint — 61

RECONNAISSANCE

- Cavalry Recon Platoon — 65

ARTILLERY

- Field Artillery Battery — 72
- Provisional Artillery Battery — 73
- Rocket Launcher Battery — 75

ARTILLERY

- Calliope Tank Platoon — 54
- Chemical Mortar Platoon — 55
- Field Artillery Battery — 72
- Rocket Launcher Battery — 75

ARTILLERY

- Field Artillery Battery — 72
- Field Artillery Battery (155mm) — 72
- Armored Field Artillery Battery — 74
- Field Artillery Battery (155mm Gun SP) — 75

ANTI-AIRCRAFT

- Anti-aircraft Artillery Platoon — 76
- Heavy Anti-aircraft Artillery Platoon — 76
- Anti-aircraft Artillery (Self-propelled) Platoon — 77

AIRCRAFT

- Air Support — 77
- Air Observation Post — 77

RIFLE COMPANY

MOTIVATION AND SKILL

A Rifle Company from the 2nd Infantry Division is rated **Confident Veteran**.

A Rifle Company from the 99th Infantry Division is rated **Confident Trained**.

2ND INFANTRY DIVISION
RELUCTANT	CONSCRIPT
CONFIDENT	TRAINED
FEARLESS	VETERAN

99TH INFANTRY DIVISION
RELUCTANT	CONSCRIPT
CONFIDENT	TRAINED
FEARLESS	VETERAN

HEADQUARTERS

RIFLE COMPANY HQ

HEADQUARTERS

| Company HQ | 15 points (2nd) | 10 points (99th) |

OPTIONS
- Replace all Command Carbine teams with Command SMG teams for +10 points per team.
- Add up to three Sniper teams for +50 points per team.

RIFLE COMPANY HQ
- CAPTAIN
  - Company Command Carbine team
  - 2iC Command Carbine team
- COMPANY HQ

COMBAT PLATOONS

RIFLE PLATOON

PLATOON

HQ Section with:

	2nd	99th
3 Rifle Squads	200 points	155 points
2 Rifle Squads	145 points	110 points

OPTIONS
- Replace Command Rifle team with a Command SMG team for +5 points.
- Replace up to one team in any or all Rifle Squads with a Bazooka team for +5 points per Bazooka team.
- ★ Replace all Rifle teams with SMG teams for +5 points per Rifle Squad.

RIFLE PLATOON
- LIEUTENANT
  - Command Rifle team
  - Bazooka team
  - HQ SECTION
- SERGEANT
  - Rifle team, Rifle team, Rifle team — RIFLE SQUAD
- SERGEANT
  - Rifle team, Rifle team, Rifle team — RIFLE SQUAD
- SERGEANT
  - Rifle team, Rifle team, Rifle team — RIFLE SQUAD

The GIs (derived from 'General Issue', a nickname for US soldiers) of the rifle platoons form the core of your company. These 'dog faces' were well trained and some have seen combat. They are also well known for their scrounging capabilities, augmenting their platoons with unauthorised weapons such as bazookas and submachine-guns stripped from transport vehicles. While strictly against the rules, the GIs know better than others that they'll need the added firepower in the coming campaigns.

The triangular formation of an infantry division means that you can count on three rifle platoons in your company. This gives you flexibility to keep one platoon in reserve while the others hold the line.

Weapons Platoon

Platoon

HQ Section with Mortar Section and:

	★	▦
2 Machine-gun Sections	160 points	120 points
1 Machine-gun Section	115 points	90 points

Option
- Add Jeep with .50 cal AA MG for +5 points.

Weapons Platoons may make Combat Attachments to Rifle Platoons.

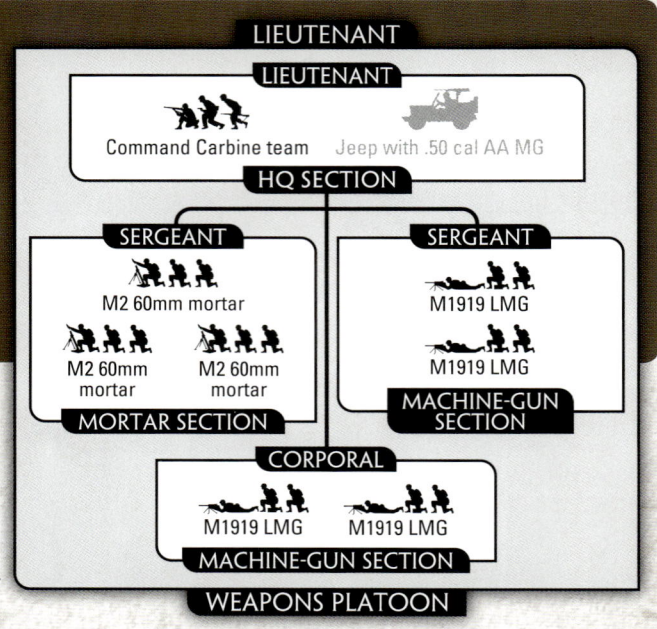

The typical weapons platoon has a mortar and a machine-gun section but, like the GIs from the rifle platoons, your men have been known to acquire a second machine-gun section through 'midnight requisition' to bolster their rate of fire. Use these machine-guns and mortars to break-up enemy assaults before they hit your lines.

Don't forget that your 60mm mortars are excellent at digging out enemy troops and gun nests. Eliminate those threats with the mortars and use your M1919 light machine-guns as a base of fire, keeping the enemy's head down while you charge in, bayonets fixed.

WEAPONS PLATOON (diagram)

LIEUTENANT — Command Carbine team, Jeep with .50 cal AA MG — HQ SECTION

SERGEANT — M2 60mm mortar, M2 60mm mortar, M2 60mm mortar — MORTAR SECTION

SERGEANT — M1919 LMG, M1919 LMG — MACHINE-GUN SECTION

CORPORAL — M1919 LMG, M1919 LMG — MACHINE-GUN SECTION

WEAPONS PLATOONS

Machine-gun Platoon

Platoon

HQ Section with:

	★	▼	▦
2 Machine-gun Sections	130 points	-	100 points

Options
- ★ Add a Bazooka team to any or all Machine-gun Sections for +20 points per Bazooka team.
- ▦ Add a Bazooka team to any or all Machine-gun Sections for +15 points per Bazooka team.
- Add Jeep with .50 cal AA MG and Jeeps with trailers for +10 points for the platoon.

Machine-gun Platoons may make Combat Attachments to Rifle Platoons.

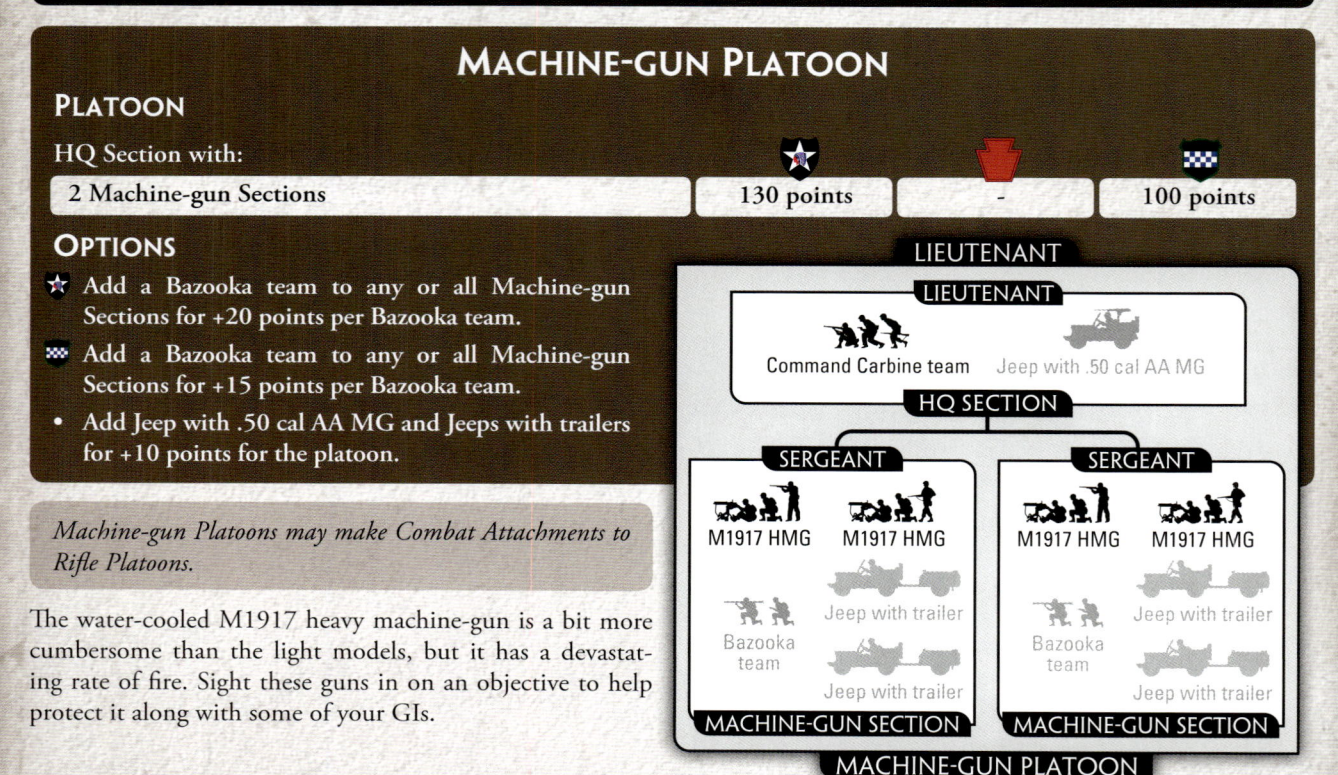

The water-cooled M1917 heavy machine-gun is a bit more cumbersome than the light models, but it has a devastating rate of fire. Sight these guns in on an objective to help protect it along with some of your GIs.

MACHINE-GUN PLATOON (diagram)

LIEUTENANT — Command Carbine team, Jeep with .50 cal AA MG — HQ SECTION

SERGEANT — M1917 HMG, M1917 HMG, Bazooka team, Jeep with trailer, Jeep with trailer — MACHINE-GUN SECTION

SERGEANT — M1917 HMG, M1917 HMG, Bazooka team, Jeep with trailer, Jeep with trailer — MACHINE-GUN SECTION

50

Mortar Platoon

Platoon

HQ Section with:

	★	🔺	▣
3 Mortar Sections	155 points	140 points	120 points
2 Mortar Sections	110 points	100 points	85 points

Options

- ★ Add a Bazooka team to any or all Mortar Sections for +20 points per Bazooka team.
- 🔺 Add a Bazooka team to any or all Mortar Sections for +15 points per Bazooka team.
- ▣ Add a Bazooka team to any or all Mortar Sections for +15 points per Bazooka team.
- Add Jeep with .50 cal AA MG and Jeeps with trailers for +10 points for the platoon.

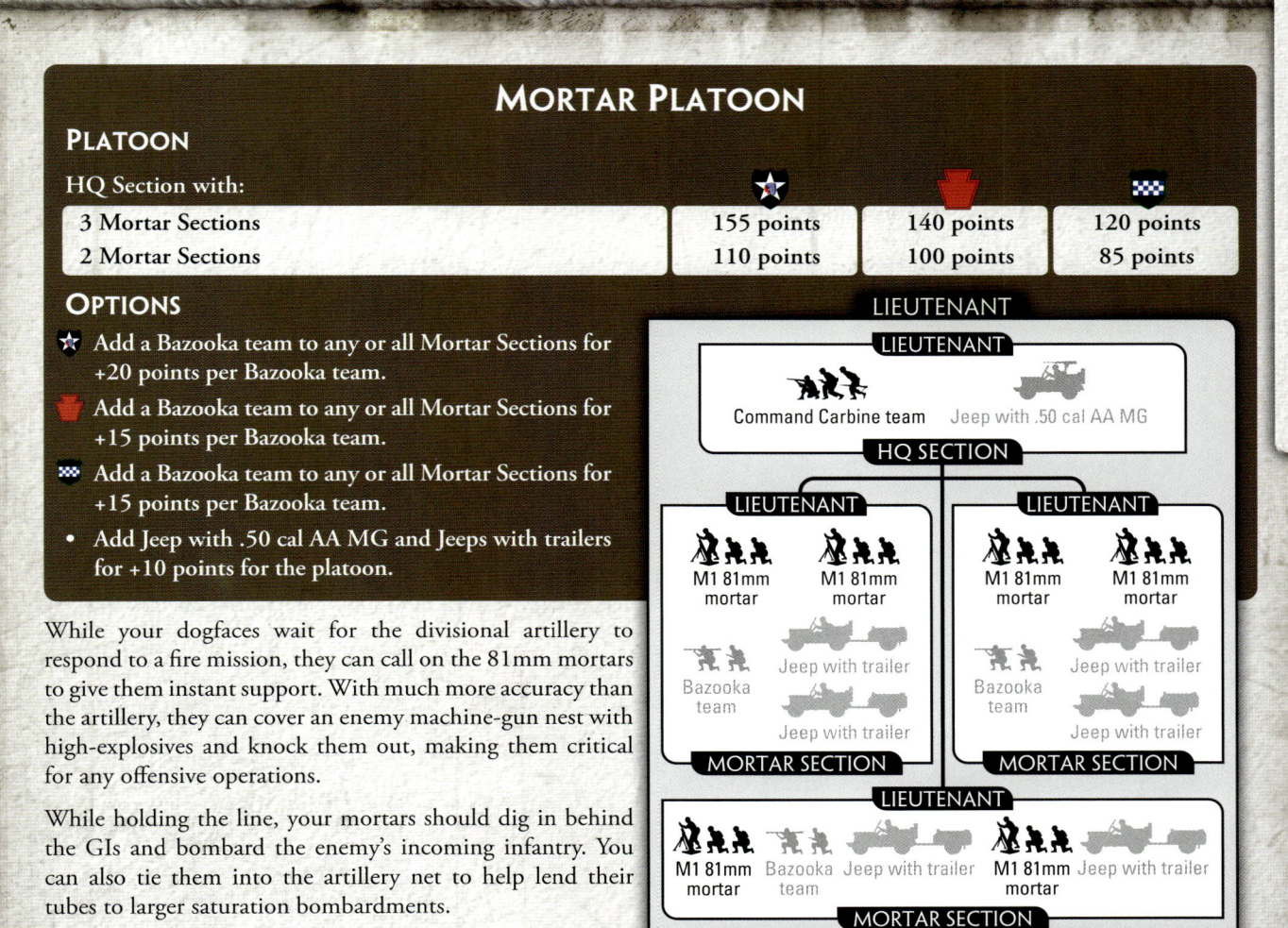

While your dogfaces wait for the divisional artillery to respond to a fire mission, they can call on the 81mm mortars to give them instant support. With much more accuracy than the artillery, they can cover an enemy machine-gun nest with high-explosives and knock them out, making them critical for any offensive operations.

While holding the line, your mortars should dig in behind the GIs and bombard the enemy's incoming infantry. You can also tie them into the artillery net to help lend their tubes to larger saturation bombardments.

Mortar Platoon

LIEUTENANT
- **HQ SECTION**: Command Carbine team, Jeep with .50 cal AA MG

LIEUTENANT — **MORTAR SECTION**: M1 81mm mortar, M1 81mm mortar, Bazooka team, Jeep with trailer, Jeep with trailer

LIEUTENANT — **MORTAR SECTION**: M1 81mm mortar, M1 81mm mortar, Bazooka team, Jeep with trailer, Jeep with trailer

LIEUTENANT — **MORTAR SECTION**: M1 81mm mortar, Bazooka team, Jeep with trailer, M1 81mm mortar, Jeep with trailer

Anti-tank Platoon

Platoon

HQ Section with:

	★	🔺	▣
3 M1 57mm (late)	100 points	95 points	80 points
3 Bazooka teams	60 points	55 points	45 points

Options

- ★ Add a Bazooka team to any or all Gun Sections for +20 points per Bazooka team.
- 🔺 Add a Bazooka team to any or all Gun Sections for +15 points per Bazooka team.
- ▣ Add a Bazooka team to any or all Gun Sections for +15 points per Bazooka team.
- Add Jeep with .50 cal AA MG and 1½-ton trucks for +10 points for the platoon.

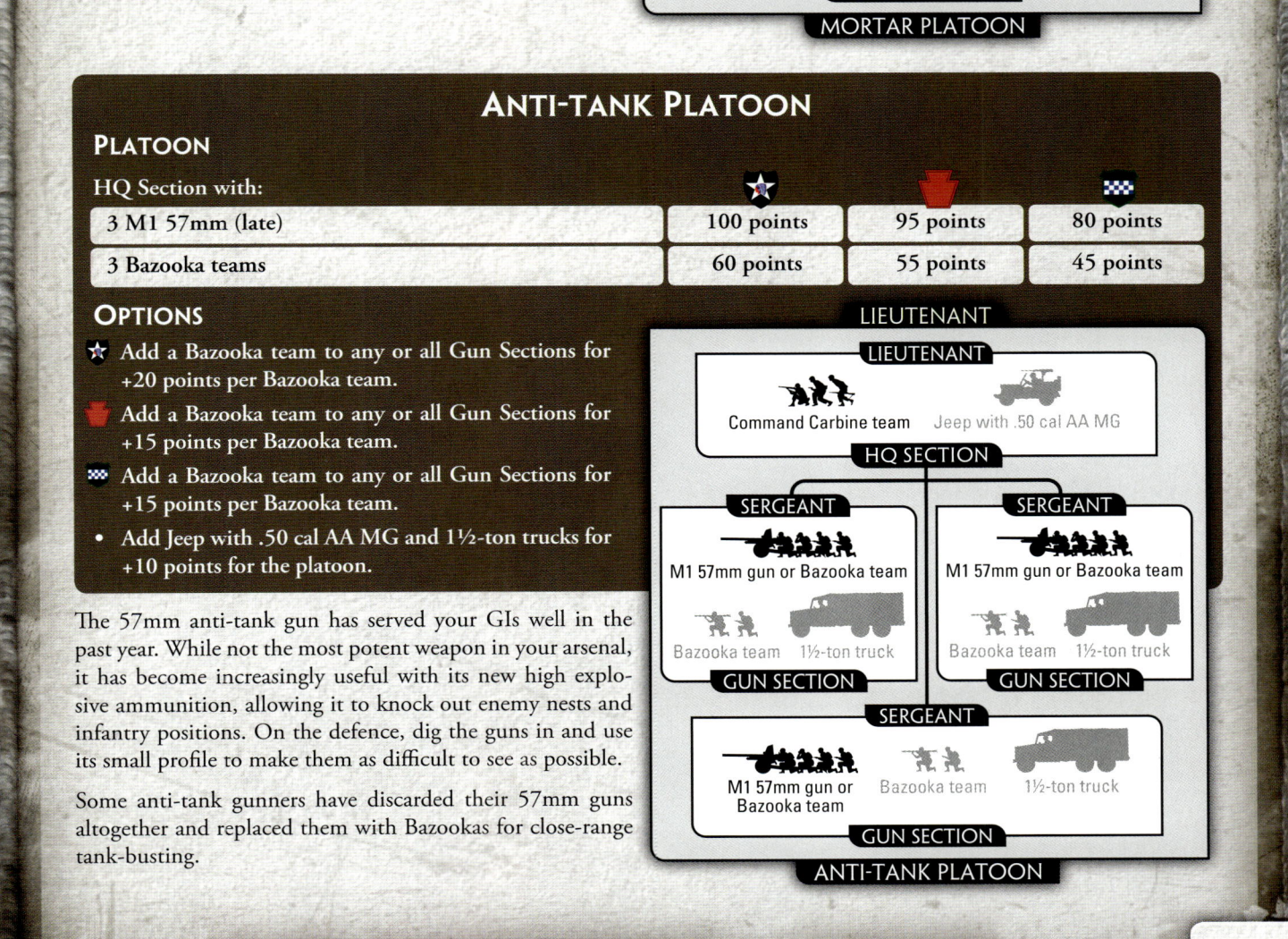

The 57mm anti-tank gun has served your GIs well in the past year. While not the most potent weapon in your arsenal, it has become increasingly useful with its new high explosive ammunition, allowing it to knock out enemy nests and infantry positions. On the defence, dig the guns in and use its small profile to make them as difficult to see as possible.

Some anti-tank gunners have discarded their 57mm guns altogether and replaced them with Bazookas for close-range tank-busting.

Anti-tank Platoon

LIEUTENANT
- **HQ SECTION**: Command Carbine team, Jeep with .50 cal AA MG

SERGEANT — **GUN SECTION**: M1 57mm gun or Bazooka team, Bazooka team, 1½-ton truck

SERGEANT — **GUN SECTION**: M1 57mm gun or Bazooka team, Bazooka team, 1½-ton truck

SERGEANT — **GUN SECTION**: M1 57mm gun or Bazooka team, Bazooka team, 1½-ton truck

Rifle Company

Ammunition & Pioneer Platoon

Platoon

HQ Section with:

3 A&P Squads	165 points	125 points	125 points
2 A&P Squads	115 points	90 points	90 points

Options

- ★ Add up to two Bazooka teams for +20 points per Bazooka team.
- ▼ Add up to two Bazooka teams for +15 points per Bazooka team.
- ▣ Add up to two Bazooka teams for +15 points per Bazooka team.
- Add Pioneer Supply truck for +25 points.

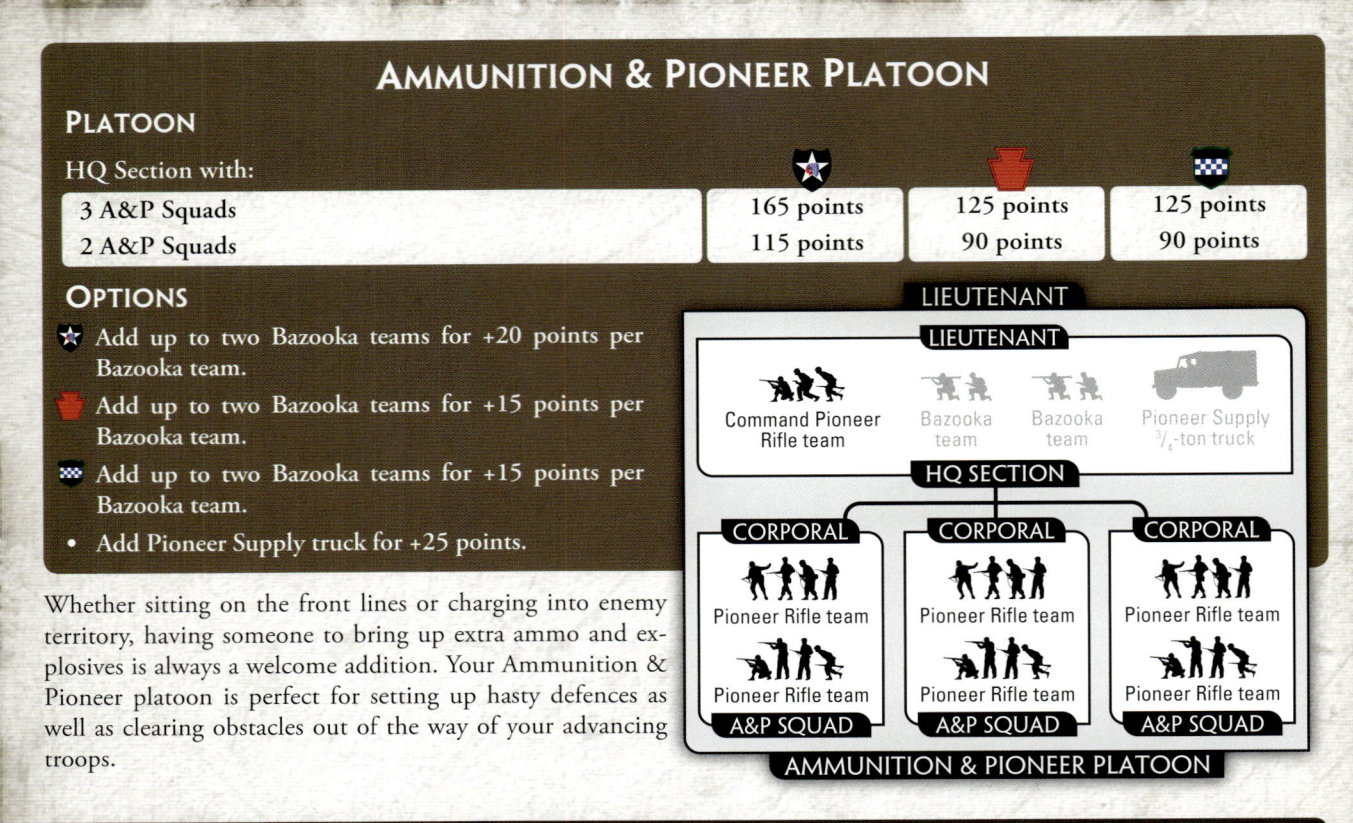

Whether sitting on the front lines or charging into enemy territory, having someone to bring up extra ammo and explosives is always a welcome addition. Your Ammunition & Pioneer platoon is perfect for setting up hasty defences as well as clearing obstacles out of the way of your advancing troops.

REGIMENTAL SUPPORT PLATOONS

Intelligence & Recon Platoon

Platoon

HQ Section with:

3 I&R Squads	85 points	75 points	65 points

Options

- Replace Command .50 cal Recon Jeeps with an Armored .50 cal Recon Jeep for +10 points.
- Replace up to one Recon Jeep with a Bazooka Recon Jeep for +5 points.
- Replace any or all Recon Jeeps with any combination of: .50 cal Recon Jeeps for +5 points per jeep, Armored Recon Jeeps for +10 points per jeep, and Armored .50 cal Recon Jeeps for +15 points per jeep.

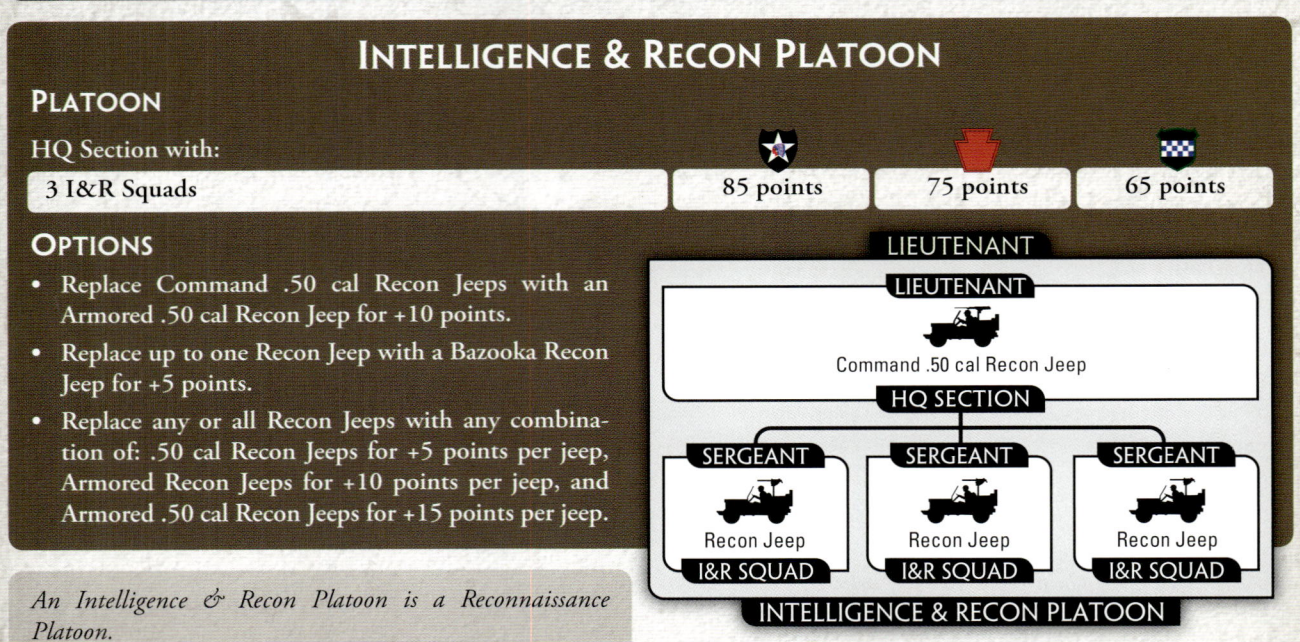

An Intelligence & Recon Platoon is a Reconnaissance Platoon.

Dismount

Before deployment you may choose to dismount all of your jeeps. If you do this, all of the platoon's vehicles are permanently removed from the game. Replace each:

- Recon Jeep or Armoured Recon Jeep with a Rifle or M1919 LMG team.
- .50 cal Recon Jeep or Armoured .50 cal Recon Jeep with a Rifle or .50 cal MG team.
- Bazooka Recon Jeep with a Rifle or Bazooka team.

Designate one of the teams as the Platoon Command team. The platoon remains a Reconnaissance Platoon.

Lieutenant Lyle Bouck's Intelligence and Reconnaissance Platoon of the 99th Infantry Division was stationed in Lanzerath. On 16 December, the 18 men of the platoon and four artillery observers ambushed the inexperienced 9th Battalion, *3. Fallschirmjägerdivision* (3rd Parachute Division) from fortified positions. It wasn't until dusk that the Germans finally captured the American platoon. While nearly all of the Americans were wounded, remarkably only one was killed. For their effort Bouck's platoon had killed 16 and wounded 63 Germans (13 more were missing), but more importantly, they had halted the *Fallschirmjäger* and the entire *1. SS-Panzerdivision* for over 20 hours.

RIFLE COMPANY

CANNON PLATOON

PLATOON

HQ Section with:

	★	🚩	◈
6 M3 105mm	205 points	180 points	155 points
4 M3 105mm	140 points	125 points	105 points

OPTION

- Add Jeeps and 1½-ton trucks for +5 points for the platoon.

The cannon platoon is your regiment's very own artillery battery. With six light howitzers on call, your GIs can rely on quality bombardments that can cover a large area.

The 105mm shells are not only exceptionally good at digging out enemy troops, they won't dilute bombardments when coordinating with your divisional artillery. This means that if you tie your cannon platoon into your divisional artillery nets, you can expect to see one hell of a fireworks display over the heads of your enemy!

CANNON PLATOON

HQ SECTION — CAPTAIN
- Command Carbine team
- Jeep
- Observer Carbine team
- Jeep

GUN SECTION — LIEUTENANT
- M3 105mm light howitzer
- 1½-ton truck
- M3 105mm light howitzer
- 1½-ton truck

GUN SECTION — LIEUTENANT
- M3 105mm light howitzer
- 1½-ton truck
- M3 105mm light howitzer
- 1½-ton truck

GUN SECTION — LIEUTENANT
- M3 105mm light howitzer
- 1½-ton truck
- M3 105mm light howitzer
- 1½-ton truck

RIFLE COMPANY SUPPORT PLATOONS

MOTIVATION AND SKILL

Divisional, corps, and army support came in all sorts of shapes and sizes during the confused battle of the Ardennes. In fact, in the confusion of battle, you might even find support from another division before your own!

Veteran Support
RELUCTANT	CONSCRIPT
CONFIDENT	TRAINED
FEARLESS	**VETERAN**

Trained Support
RELUCTANT	CONSCRIPT
CONFIDENT	**TRAINED**
FEARLESS	VETERAN

CALLIOPE TANK PLATOON

PLATOON

4 T34 Calliope	160 points
3 T34 Calliope	125 points
2 T34 Calliope	80 points

OPTION
- Fit any or all tanks with Improvised Armour for +5 points for the platoon.

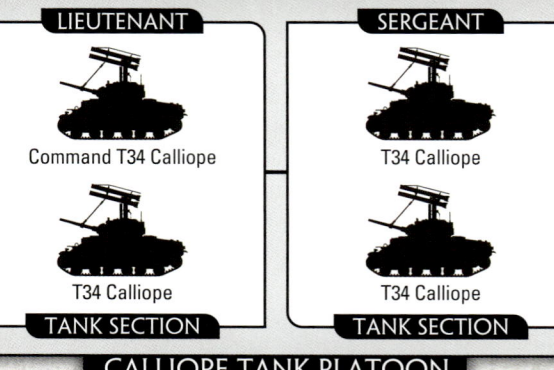

> T34 Calliope teams may not Charge into Contact and must Break Off rather than Counterattack if Assaulted (see pages 144 and 165 of the rulebook).

LIEUTENANT

Lieutenant — Command T34 Calliope / T34 Calliope (Tank Section)

Sergeant — T34 Calliope / T34 Calliope (Tank Section)

CALLIOPE TANK PLATOON

The 30th and 90th Infantry Divisions' 743rd and 712th Tank Battalions were among the first to receive T34 Calliope rocket launcher kits. These launchers were named after the Calliope (pronounced Kal-lee-ohp by some and Kal-lie-oh-pee by others) steam-powered organ played at carnivals and circuses. The launcher's frame couldn't stand up to the main gun's recoil, so the crews became dedicated rocketeers, forgoing their main gun completely.

CALLIOPE ROCKET LAUNCHER RULES

SATURATION BOMBARDMENT

Each Calliope rocket launcher system fired a bombardment of sixty 4.5" (114mm) rockets. Individually, these rockets may not cause much damage, but group 60 to 240 of them into a single salvo and the enemy will have nowhere to hide!

Calliope launcher kits were attached to tanks from an infantry division's tank battalion. This meant that the Calliope crews were full-time tankers but only part-time artillerymen without much, if any, specialised training.

> Each T34 Calliope counts as four weapons when firing an Artillery Bombardment.
>
> A Calliope Tank Platoon cannot use the Hit 'Em With Everything You Got special rule.

SIXTY ROCKETS

The Calliope's 60 rocket tubes took a bit of time to reload, but a crack crew found ways to speed things up for the next salvo.

> At the start of the game, place a Full Salvo marker with a platoon with Sixty Rockets rocket launchers. Remove this marker after firing an Artillery Bombardment.
>
> If a platoon with Sixty Rockets rocket launchers does not have a Full Salvo marker when it fires an Artillery Bombardment, roll a Skill Test for each Rocket Launcher able to fire in the Bombardment. Only those that pass the Skill Test can fire as part of the Bombardment.
>
> Place a Full Salvo marker on a platoon with Sixty Rockets rocket launchers at the end of any Shooting Step in which every Rocket Launcher in the platoon was able to fire an Artillery Bombardment, but none did so.

RIFLE COMPANY

SCRAPYARD TANK PLATOON

PLATOON

5 Scrapyard Tanks	see below
4 Scrapyard Tanks	see below
3 Scrapyard Tanks	see below

The Scrapyard Tanks in this platoon must be chosen from the following:

- up to three M4 or M4A1 Sherman for +65 points per tank.
- up to three M5A1 Stuart for +40 points per tank.
- up to two M24 Chaffee for +65 points per tank.
- up to two M7 Priest HMC for +25 points per tank.
- up to two M4 (105mm) Sherman for +45 points.
- up to one M8 Scott HMC for +30 points per tank.
- up to one M12 155mm GMC for +55 points.
- up to one M36 90mm GMC for +75 points.
- up to one M10 3in GMC (late) for +65 points.

LIEUTENANT
Command Scrapyard Tank
HQ SECTION

SERGEANT — Scrapyard Tank, Scrapyard Tank — **TANK SECTION**

SERGEANT — Scrapyard Tank, Scrapyard Tank — **TANK SECTION**

SCRAPYARD TANK PLATOON

Teams from a Scrapyard Tank Platoon cannot fire Artillery Bombardments.

The 740th 'Daredevils' Tank Battalion arrived at the front with no tanks whatsoever and the few Shermans their commanding officer, Lt. Colonel George Rubel, had scrounged up were taken to reinforce other tank battalions. So the Daredevils salvaged whatever they could from local repair depots, including 15 M4 Shermans, several M5A1 Stuarts, two M4 105mm assault guns, an M8 Scott assault gun, two M24 Chaffee light tanks, two Sherman DD tanks, a few M7 105mm self-propelled howitzers, and some M10 and M36 tank destroyers. Using this weird array of equipment, the platoon commanders were allowed to construct their platoons as they saw fit.

The battalion joined the 30th Infantry Division and went into action to help stop *SS-Kampfgruppe Peiper* near Stoumont. During the fighting at La Gleize, Rubel added an M12 155mm self-propelled gun to the battalion, which poured over 190 devastating rounds into Peiper's battlegroup bottled up in the village.

CHEMICAL MORTAR PLATOON

PLATOON

HQ Section with:

	V	T
2 Mortar Sections	160 points	120 points
1 Mortar Section	95 points	70 points

OPTIONS

- V Add up to one Bazooka team per Mortar Section for +20 points per Bazooka team.
- T Add up to one Bazooka team per Mortar Section for +15 points per Bazooka team.
- Add Jeep with .50 cal AA MG and Jeeps with trailers for +10 points for the platoon.

LIEUTENANT
Command Carbine team, Jeep with .50 cal AA MG, Observer Carbine team
HQ SECTION

SERGEANT — 4.2" chemical mortar, 4.2" chemical mortar, Bazooka team, Jeep with trailer, Jeep with trailer — **MORTAR SECTION**

SERGEANT — 4.2" chemical mortar, 4.2" chemical mortar, Bazooka team, Jeep with trailer, Jeep with trailer — **MORTAR SECTION**

CHEMICAL MORTAR PLATOON

Chemical mortars have all of the advantages of mortars, a quick response and accurate results, plus, they have the firepower of a 105mm howitzer. This makes them ideal for supporting your infantry assaults and breaking up enemy attacks.

55

THE DAMNED ENGINEERS!
THE 291ST ENGINEER COMBAT BATTALION

The 291st Engineer Combat Battalion was formed in April 1943. After intense training, Lieutenant Colonel David E Pergrin was given command of the battalion. In October 1943 they moved to England where they built the camps and roads for the Allied invasion force.

Normandy

The battalion arrived in France on 23 June 1944 and immediately went to work clearing and maintaining the roads around Carentan. In July, the battalion saw its first front-line combat when they helped pickaxe, bulldoze, and blast through the hellish bocage landscape of Normandy. After the bloody hedgerow fighting, the 291st 'liberated' many of the abandoned vehicles left by the Germans around Mortain to add to their motor pool.

The German Frontier

The 291st joined the 51st and 202nd Combat Engineer Battalions, forming the 1111th Engineer Group attached to the US V Corps. The group followed in the charge across France, rebuilding bridges destroyed by the Germans.

December 1944 found the 291st sprawled across a large but relatively quiet sector in Belgium. Elements were stationed in Malmédy, Stavelot, La Gleize, and Trois-Ponts among other smaller outposts. As far as the engineers knew, they were safely tucked away behind the 106th Infantry Division, several miles back from the front lines.

Battle of the Bulge

Like other US forces in the Ardennes, the German attack left the engineers isolated from V Corps and on their own. Confused and often conflicting reports drifted into Colonel Pergrin's headquarters, but he quickly worked out that the Germans were up to something big. He collected his battalion from their remote outposts and established roadblocks at key locations such as Stavelot, La Gleize, Trois-Ponts, Amblève, and Malmédy.

Soon, the engineers had platoons of the shattered 106th Infantry Division and the counter-attacking 7th Armored Division passing through their position. Pergrin pleaded in vain with both divisions to spare men to stay and help defend the town. None stayed, however he did inherit several abandoned anti-tank guns, a vital boost to his force that had minimal anti-tank assets.

Malmédy Massacre

At noon on 17 December a column of 140 men from the 285th Field Artillery Battery Observation Battalion, attached to the 7th Armored, ran into one of Pergrin's roadblocks. The artillerymen ignored warnings that the enemy was operating in the area, and pushed on. Then, between 1530 hours and midnight, 17 wounded survivors limped their way back to the 291st. After debriefing the survivors, Pergin learned that observers had run into Peiper's column and after a quick firefight they surrendered. Then suddenly, Peiper's men opened fire on the prisoners of war, killing 84 of them in cold blood. Pergrin quickly dispatched patrols to the site to collect more survivors and then reported the incident to Allied command.

Stavelot

At 1930 hours, 17 December, Peiper's leading panzers approached one of the hidden roadblocks manned by Sergeant Chuck Hensel's squad from C Company. The men had set up daisy chains of several mines tied together by a rope, which could be pulled across the road in front of approaching panzers. As the Panthers moved closer, one of the engineers let loose a bazooka round which smashed harmlessly into the front of the leading tank. The Germans hesitated and withdrew, thinking the road was heavily defended. In actual fact, only Hensel and his few engineers stood between them and the vital Stavelot bridge!

Meanwhile, two companies of armoured infantry and four 3" anti-tank guns took up defensive positions in Stavelot. After a short fight, the Germans managed to storm the bridge and bypass the bulk of the American defenders. Thinking Stavelot was secured, Peiper carried on pushing west.

THE BRIDGES AND THE DAMNED ENGINEERS

THE DAMNED ENGINEERS

Trois Ponts

From Stavelot, he sent a small force of Panzer IV tanks and pioneers to Wanne to capture a crossing south of his next objective. His own troops focused on the Trois Ponts.

Separated by the Amblève River, the two forces closed on their objectives, but Pergrin's engineers were one step ahead of them and both bridges were sent into oblivion with TNT just as the panzers approached. Peiper's southern task force had to return all of the way back to Stavelot in order to cross the Amblève and rejoin the main force, wasting precious fuel. Peiper's own force abandoned Trois Ponts and wandered north along the Amblève looking for a suitable crossing.

Habiémont

Frustrated, Peiper found a hidden crossing overlooked by the engineers and finally crossed the river. However, Peiper's new position was given away by an intense fighter-bomber attack which alerted the engineers. There was only one place Peiper could be going: Habiémont.

A truckload of TNT arrived just in time at Habiémont bridge, and once again as the panzers approached, the bridge exploded. Peiper slammed his fist on his Panther and exclaimed, "The damned engineers. The damned engineers!"

Malmédy

As Peiper's column sped beyond the reach of the 291st, help arrived at Malmédy. Two 90mm anti-aircraft guns, the 99th Infantry Battalion (Separate), the 526th Armored Infantry Battalion, and the 825th Tank Destroyer Battalion bolstered the engineers just in time as Otto Skorzeny's *150. Panzerbrigade* attacked on 21 December. The 99th held the line, while the engineers manned roadblocks and set up ambushes, helping to repel Skorzeny's assault. After Malmédy, the 291st joined the rest of the V Corps in eradicating the 'bulge', rebuilding bridges and paving the way.

To Victory

By war's end, the 291st had made seven river assaults and constructed 74 bridges, 11 of which were built under fire, including a record setting 1000-foot (300m) bridge built at Remagen in 32 hours. For their actions, the 291st was awarded a Presidential Unit Citation.

291ST ENGINEER COMBAT BATTALION SPECIAL RULES

An Engineer Combat Company uses all of the normal US special rules found on pages 236 to 240 of the rulebook. In addition, they also use the Boy Scouts, Why We Fight, and Eightballs, Oddballs, and Screwballs special rules.

Boy Scouts

Over 80% of the battalion were former members of the Boy Scouts. The old scout motto 'Be Prepared' certainly gave rise to clever booby traps that helped stall Peiper's charge.

Instead of placing a Minefield or three Barbed Wire Entanglements for a Pioneer Supply Truck (see page 263 of the rulebook), you may instead place up to three Booby Traps (see page 230 of the rulebook).

Why We Fight

The 291st Engineer Combat Battalion had the sad duty of collecting survivors of the Malmédy Massacre and reporting the incident to headquarters.

All Americans platoons from a company with the Why We Fight special rule use the British Bulldog rule (see page 246 of the rulebook) in Assaults involving any SS platoons.

Eightballs, Oddballs, and Screwballs

The engineers ranged from well-educated civil engineers to self-taught mechanics and Colonel Pergrin made sure that they all knew the score and no one was left in the dark.

Engineer Combat Platoons use the German Mission Tactics special rules on page 242 of the rulebook.

57

ENGINEER COMBAT COMPANY
INFANTRY COMPANY

Motivation and Skill

The highly trained 1111th Engineer Combat Group was galvanised in the bloody hedgerow fighting in Normandy. An Engineer Combat Company is rated **Confident Veteran**.

RELUCTANT	CONSCRIPT
CONFIDENT	TRAINED
FEARLESS	**VETERAN**

HEADQUARTERS

- Engineer Combat Company HQ — 59

You must field one platoon from each box shaded black and may field one platoon from each box shaded grey.

Support platoons can be of any variant type and do not have to match your Company HQ.

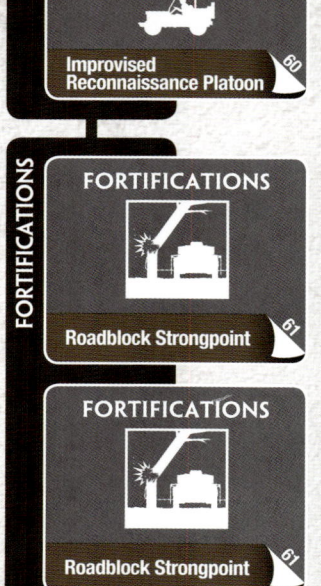

COMBAT PLATOONS

INFANTRY
- Engineer Combat Platoon — 59

INFANTRY
- Engineer Combat Platoon — 59

INFANTRY
- Engineer Combat Platoon — 59

WEAPONS PLATOONS

MACHINE-GUNS
- Improvised Machine-gun Platoon — 60

RECONNAISSANCE
- Improvised Reconnaissance Platoon — 60

FORTIFICATIONS

FORTIFICATIONS
- Roadblock Strongpoint — 61

FORTIFICATIONS
- Roadblock Strongpoint — 61

SUPPORT PLATOONS

ARMOUR
- Tank Platoon — 68
- Tank Destroyer Platoon — 69
- Towed Tank Destroyer Platoon — 69

INFANTRY OR ANTI-TANK
- Armored Rifle Platoon — 70
- Rifle Platoon — 49
- Armored Anti-tank Platoon — 70
- Parachute Rifle Platoon — 71

INFANTRY
- Armored Rifle Platoon — 70
- Rifle Platoon — 49
- Parachute Rifle Platoon — 71

ARTILLERY
- Field Artillery Battery — 72

ANTI-AIRCRAFT
- Anti-aircraft Artillery (Self-propelled) Platoon — 77
- Heavy Anti-aircraft Artillery Platoon — 76

AIRCRAFT
- Air Support — 77
- Air Observation Post — 77

HEADQUARTERS

ENGINEER COMBAT COMPANY HQ
HEADQUARTERS

| Company HQ | 15 points |

OPTIONS

- Replace either or both Command Carbine teams with Command SMG teams for +15 points per team
- Add ¾-ton truck with AA MG and Jeep with .50 cal AA MG for +10 points.
- Add up to two M1 57mm (late) anti-tank guns for +35 points per gun.
- Add up to three Bazooka teams for +20 points per team.

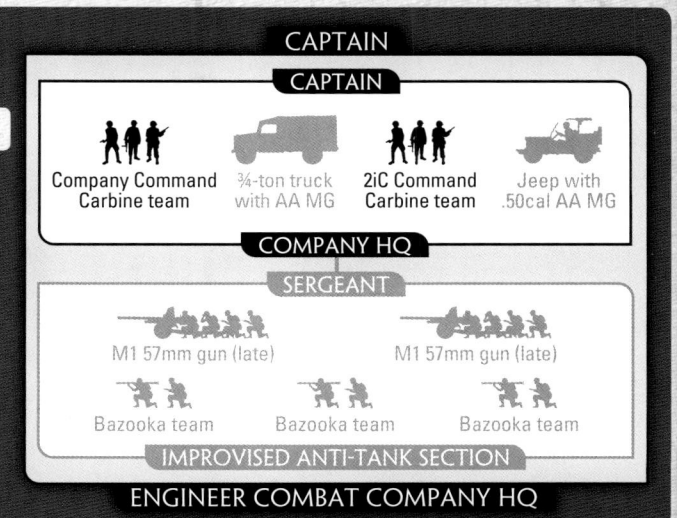

CAPTAIN

Company Command Carbine team — ¾-ton truck with AA MG — 2iC Command Carbine team — Jeep with .50cal AA MG

COMPANY HQ

SERGEANT

M1 57mm gun (late) — M1 57mm gun (late)
Bazooka team — Bazooka team — Bazooka team

IMPROVISED ANTI-TANK SECTION

ENGINEER COMBAT COMPANY HQ

When the Germans attacked, the men of the 1111th Engineer Group were the backstop of the American lines. Once through the 106th and 99th Infantry Divisions, the Germans ran head-long into the many engineer roadblocks.

To help man the defences, Colonel Pergrin's 291st Combat Engineers shifted all of A Company's bazookas to Malmédy to add more anti-tank capability to the anti-tank guns acquired from retreating infantry.

COMBAT PLATOONS

ENGINEER COMBAT PLATOON
PLATOON

HQ Section with Weapons squad and:

| 2 Operating Squads | 200 points |
| 1 Operating Squad | 150 points |

OPTIONS

- Replace Command Pioneer Rifle team with a Command Pioneer SMG team for +5 points.
- Add a Bazooka team to any or all Sections or Squads for +20 points per Bazooka team.
- Add Pioneer Supply 2½-ton dump truck for +25 points.
- Add a D7 Bulldozer for +15 points.
- Add Jeep with .50 cal AA MG and 2½-ton dump trucks for +10 points for the platoon.
- Arm any or all 2½-ton dump trucks with .50 cal AA MG for +5 points per truck.

LIEUTENANT

Command Pioneer Rifle team — Bazooka team
Jeep with .50cal AA MG — Pioneer Supply 2½-ton dump truck

HQ SECTION

SERGEANT

D7 Bulldozer

TRACTOR SECTION

SERGEANT / **SERGEANT**

Pioneer Rifle team — Pioneer Rifle team
2½-ton dump truck
Bazooka team

OPERATING SQUAD / **OPERATING SQUAD**

SERGEANT

Pioneer M1917 HMG — Pioneer M1917 HMG — 2½-ton dump truck — Bazooka team

WEAPONS SQUAD

ENGINEER COMBAT PLATOON

The combat engineers of the 1111th Engineer Combat Group found themselves to be the only thing standing between *SS-Kampfgruppe Peiper* and the Meuse River.

USING CAPTURED VEHICLES

The combat engineers of the 291st Engineer Combat Battalion made extensive use of captured German trucks and jeeps. So much so, that Colonel Pergrin worried that they might be mistaken for a German unit!

Since the only difference is a visual one, feel free to model any or all of your 2½-ton trucks with German 3-ton trucks, and any or all of your jeeps with Kübelwagen jeeps.

You may replace all Pioneer HMG teams with Pioneer Rifle teams at the start of the game before deployment.

WEAPONS PLATOONS

IMPROVISED MACHINE-GUN PLATOON

PLATOON
HQ Section with:

4 M1917	130 points
2 M1917	65 points
4 M2 .50 cal	90 points

An Improvised Machine-gun Platoon may make Combat Attachments to Combat Engineer Platoons.

Colonel Pergrin called up the M1917 machine-guns from A Company to bolster B Company holding Malmédy. The reinforcements stripped a few trucks of M2 .50 cal machine-guns and brought them along as well.

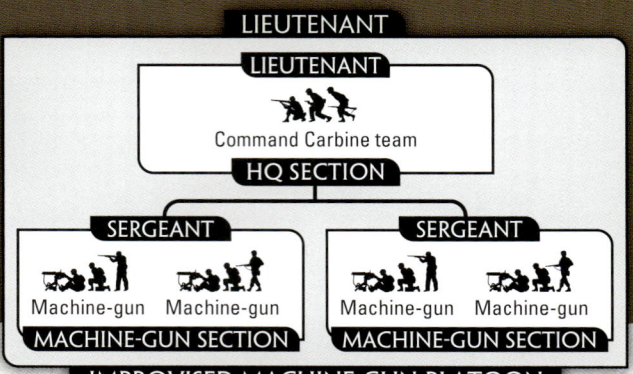

IMPROVISED RECONNAISSANCE PLATOON

PLATOON

3 Jeep Patrols	120 points
2 Jeep Patrols	80 points
1 Jeep Patrol	40 points

OPTION
- Replace any or all Recon Jeeps with .50 cal Recon Jeeps for +5 points per jeep.

Jeep Patrols from an Improvised Reconnaissance Platoon operate as separate platoons, each with their own command team.

Jeep Patrols are Reconnaissance Platoons

With absolutely no authorised reconnaissance of their own, other than the battalion's small two-jeep reconnaissance section, the engineers formed ad hoc patrols of pairs of jeeps and sent them out all across the front to keep tabs on Peiper's column and report back.

These bold patrols raced forward and quickly discovered the German tanks. Their reconnaissance was essential for the engineers to keep one step ahead of Peiper during the early critical days of the battle.

FORTIFICATIONS

ROADBLOCK STRONGPOINT
PLATOON

Roadblock Strongpoint	170 points

OPTIONS
- Add a second Operating Section for +55 points.
- Add a second Weapons Section for +90 points.
- Add a Gun Section with a M1 57mm (late) gun in a Gun Pit for +45 points or a M5 3in (late) gun in a Gun Pit for +60 points.
- Add up to one Anti-tank Obstacle for +100 points.
- Replace either or both M1917 HMG with M2 .50 cal MG for -10 points per team.

A Roadblock Strongpoint is a Fortified Platoon (see page 262 of the rulebook).

A company that includes a Roadblock Strongpoint is a Fortified Company (see pages 257 and 262 of the rulebook).

Booby Traps are Area Defences and are therefore deployed using the Placing Booby Traps rules (see page 230 of the rulebook) and do not have to deploy with the rest of the Fortified Platoon.

Roadblocks formed the core of the engineers' defence. Typically they would mine the road and its shoulders and set up trenches and gun pits covering the position. Often the weapons squad would put their .30 cal or .50 cal machine-guns into emplacements for additional protection. A few anti-tank guns were scrounged up from shattered units to give the engineers a little defence against German tanks.

They also used a series of booby traps. Anti-tank mines were daisy-chained together so that they could be dragged across the road in front of enemy tanks and half-tracks. Large trees were rigged with TNT so that when an enemy vehicle tripped a wire, the tree would fall and block the road. Even barbed wire entanglements were booby trapped with TNT and mines to inflict damage on the Germans trying to clear the way.

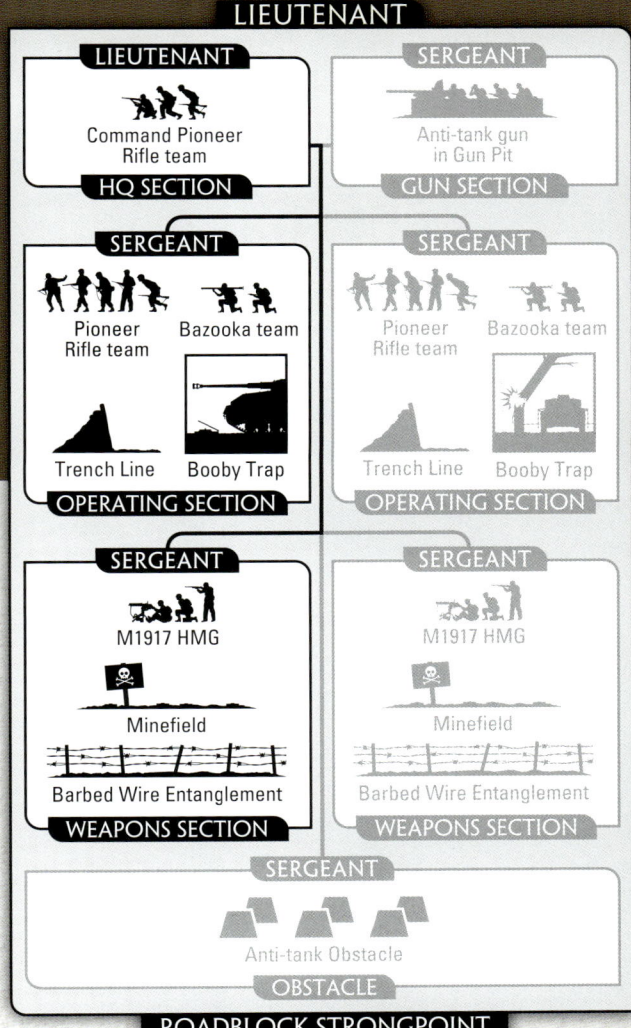

Anti-tank obstacles could be anything from dozens of felled trees to 'flaming roadblocks' where the men would fill ditches across the roads with fuel and light it on fire. In some locations in the southern sector, roadblocks were positioned along portions of the West Wall that were in American hands, making use of the large rows of dragon's teeth against the army that built them.

ROADBLOCK STRONGPOINT

- **HQ SECTION** (Lieutenant): Command Pioneer Rifle team
- **GUN SECTION** (Sergeant): Anti-tank gun in Gun Pit
- **OPERATING SECTION** (Sergeant): Pioneer Rifle team, Bazooka team, Trench Line, Booby Trap
- **OPERATING SECTION** (Sergeant): Pioneer Rifle team, Bazooka team, Trench Line, Booby Trap
- **WEAPONS SECTION** (Sergeant): M1917 HMG, Minefield, Barbed Wire Entanglement
- **WEAPONS SECTION** (Sergeant): M1917 HMG, Minefield, Barbed Wire Entanglement
- **OBSTACLE** (Sergeant): Anti-tank Obstacle

ENGINEER COMBAT COMPANY

MINDING THE GAP
THE 14TH CAVALRY GROUP

The 14th Cavalry Group, consisting of the 18th and 32nd Cavalry Squadrons, arrived in France on 27 September 1944. They were assigned to support the US VIII Corps in a defensive role in the Ardennes, covering the space between the 99th and 106th Infantry Divisions.

This region, known as the Losheim Gap, was good going for armoured forces, and as such was the most likely spot the Germans would attack. But the Allies took a calculated risk that the Germans couldn't go on the offensive after all of the Summer defeats they had sustained, even if they wanted to.

The 18th Cavalry Squadron (a battalion-strength unit) was stationed near the front in Manderfeld while the 32nd was held back in Vielsalm to rest and refit. To help with their defence, the group was given a company from the 820th Tank Destroyer Battalion (towed M5 3" anti-tank guns) and three batteries from the 275th Field Artillery Battalion equipped with 18 M7 Priests.

THE LOSHEIM GAP

In the pre-dawn hours of 16 December 1944, the full weight of *12. Volksgrenadierdivision* (12th Peoples' Grenadier Division) was thrown against the cavalrymen. Almost immediately things started to unravel for the Germans. The red signal flare sent up alerted the cavalry of the incoming attack, and the massive number of searchlights meant to show the way, simply silhouetted the men and made them easy targets.

The troops of the 18th Squadron occupying their outposts opened fire. The *Volksgrenadiere* were cut down by the hundreds until the cavalry were forced to retire for lack of ammunition. Falling back to Manderfeld, the 18th cavalry again delivered a devastating blow upon the Germans, this time with the added firepower of the 275th Field Artillery.

The 32nd Squadron was dispatched from Vielsalm to reinforce the 18th at Manderfeld. The squadron's E Troop were the first to arrive with six M8 Scott HMC assault guns. The Scotts quickly tied into the 275th Field Artillery's network and joined in the havoc being wrought on the *Volksgrenadiere*.

BREAKING POINT

The cavalry sent a few patrols to get an idea of the scope of the attack, which was quickly established as a large assault. The group's commander, Colonel Mark Devine raced back to the 106th Infantry Division's headquarters to request artillery support, but found the divisional staff was in a shambles and Devine returned empty handed.

By the next day, two of the 32nd Squadron's troops had been destroyed fighting *SS-Kampfgruppe Hansen*. Colonel Devine broke down and gave up command to his executive officer, Lieutenant Colonel Augustine Dugan. The new commander's life was made harder by the unreasonable demands from the 106th Infantry to retake the village of Born, something well beyond the ability of his unit. Nevertheless, Dugan gathered his shattered unit and formed a small task force. Task Force Mayes's attack with four M5A1 Stuart light tanks, a platoon of M8 Scott assault guns, and C Troop (32nd Cavalry) was valiant but unsuccessful.

The 14th Cavalry Group, now well and truly spent, was transferred to the 7th Armored. Now fully supported by the weight of the tanks and armoured infantry, the remnants of the 18th Cavalry played a useful role in the 7th Armored's excellent defence of Saint Vith and helped cover the fighting withdrawal back to Vielsalm.

Refit

In January 1945, the 18th was brought back up to full strength and were among the first to receive the new M24 Chaffee light tank to replace their aging M5A1 Stuarts. This excellent new tank combined speed and firepower, giving the cavalry the perfect tool to exact revenge upon the Germans for their fallen comrades.

Despite their losses, the 18th Cavalry managed to stall the German attack in Losheim for nearly 24 hours and in the process blunt the attacks of *12. Volksgrenadierdivision* and *3. Fallschirmjägerdivision*. For their actions during the war, they received a Presidential Unit Citation.

PATTON'S GHOSTS: THE 2ND CAVALRY GROUP

The 2nd Cavalry Group, consisting of the 2nd and 42nd Cavalry Squadrons, arrived in France in June 1944. Ordered to join Task Force A in Brittany, the group was instead intercepted and adopted by the 4th Armored Division as it raced through Brittany and on to the Moselle in the Lorraine.

As a part of XII Corps of Patton's Third Army, the 2nd Cavalry screened the right flank. On 18 September 1944, the group clashed with *111. Panzerbrigade* at Lunéville. Although they lost a large number of vehicles there, the fight stalled the Germans long enough for the 704th Tank Destroyer and 37th Tank Battalions to counter their advance. The veteran cavalrymen continued to fight alongside the 4th Armored all of the way through the Ardennes fighting. They too were among the first units to receive the new M24 Chaffee light tank to replace their loses at Lunéville and put them to good use in the field.

The group's speed, cunning, and elusiveness earned them the nickname 'Patton's Ghosts'.

CAVALRY SPECIAL RULES

A Cavalry Recon Troop and a Light Tank Company use all of the normal US special rules found on pages 236 to 240 of the rulebook. In addition, they also use the Never Out Of Touch and Why We Fight special rules.

Never Out Of Touch

The cavalry's long-range radios and high mobility of their vehicles meant that they could respond quickly to enemy threats.

> Once each turn, you may re-roll one die to receive Reserves for your force.
>
> In a mission using the Scattered Reserves special rule, once per turn you may also re-roll one die rolled to determine where a platoon will arrive from Scattered Reserve.

Why We Fight

News of the infamous Malmédy Massacre spread fast, due in no small part to Eisenhower's order to make the incident public. From that moment on, the men gave no quarter to the notorious Waffen-SS.

> All American platoons from a company with the Why We Fight special rule use the British Bulldog rule (see page 246 of the rulebook) in all Assaults involving any SS platoons.

CAVALRY RECON TROOP
MECHANISED COMPANY

MOTIVATION AND SKILL

A Cavalry Recon Troop from the 2nd Cavalry Group is rated **Confident Veteran**.

A Cavalry Recon Troop from the 14th Cavalry Group is rated **Confident Trained**.

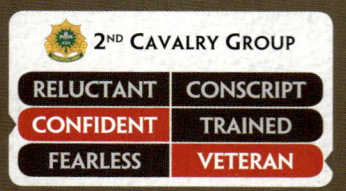

2ND CAVALRY GROUP

RELUCTANT	CONSCRIPT
CONFIDENT	TRAINED
FEARLESS	**VETERAN**

14TH CAVALRY GROUP

RELUCTANT	CONSCRIPT
CONFIDENT	**TRAINED**
FEARLESS	VETERAN

HEADQUARTERS

HEADQUARTERS
Cavalry Recon Troop HQ — 65

You must field one platoon from each box shaded black and may field one platoon from each box shaded grey.

Your Troop HQ must be either from the 2nd Cavalry Group (marked 🛡) or the 14th Cavalry Group (marked ⚐). All Combat and Weapons platoons marked with either of these symbols must be from the same cavalry group as your Company HQ. Support platoons can be of any variant type and do not have to match your Troop HQ.

COMBAT PLATOONS

RECONNAISSANCE — Cavalry Recon Platoon — 65

RECONNAISSANCE — Cavalry Recon Platoon — 65

RECONNAISSANCE — Cavalry Recon Platoon — 65

WEAPONS PLATOONS

ARMOUR — Light Tank Platoon — 67

ARMOUR — Light Tank Platoon — 67

ARTILLERY — Assault Gun Battery — 65

SUPPORT PLATOONS

ARMOUR OR ANTI-TANK
- Tank Platoon — 68
- Tank Destroyer Platoon — 69
- Towed Tank Destroyer Platoon — 69

ANTI-TANK
- Towed Tank Destroyer Platoon — 69

INFANTRY
- Rifle Platoon — 49
- Armored Rifle Platoon — 70
- Engineer Combat Platoon — 59

ARTILLERY
- Field Artillery Battery — 72
- Armored Field Artillery Battery — 74
- Provisional Artillery Battery — 73

ARTILLERY
- Armored Field Artillery Battery — 74

AIRCRAFT
- Air Support — 77
- Air Observation Post — 77

CAVALRY RECON TROOP

HEADQUARTERS

Cavalry Recon Troop HQ
Headquarters

Company HQ with:

2 M8 Greyhound	85 points	65 points

Teams from the Cavalry Recon Troop HQ are Recce teams.

CAPTAIN
- Company Command M8 armored car
- 2iC Command M8 armored car

COMPANY HQ
CAVALRY RECON TROOP HQ

COMBAT PLATOONS

Cavalry Recon Platoon
Platoon

HQ Section with:

3 Cavalry Recon Patrols	270 points	210 points
2 Cavalry Recon Patrols	180 points	140 points
1 Cavalry Recon Patrol	90 points	70 points

Dismount

Before deployment you may choose to dismount all of your Cavalry Recon Platoons. If you do this, all of the Cavalry Recon Patrols from the same platoon operate as a single platoon.

If you dismount, all of the platoon's vehicles are permanently removed from the game. Replace all of the vehicles in each Patrol with any two of the following teams for each Patrol:

- Carbine teams
- M1919 LMG teams
- up to one M2 .50 cal MG team per Cavalry Recon Patrol.
- up to one Bazooka team per Cavalry Recon Patrol.
- up to one M2 60mm mortar team per Cavalry Recon Patrol.

Designate any one of the teams as the Platoon Command team. The platoon remains a Reconnaissance Platoon.

LIEUTENANT
- Command M8 armored car
- Mortar Jeep
- Recon Jeep

CAVALRY RECON PATROL

SERGEANT
- Command M8 armored car
- Mortar Jeep
- Recon Jeep

CAVALRY RECON PATROL

SERGEANT
- Command M8 armored car
- Mortar Jeep
- Recon Jeep

CAVALRY RECON PATROL
CAVALRY RECON PLATOON

Cavalry Recon Patrols are Reconnaissance Platoons.

Cavalry Recon Patrols from Cavalry Recon Platoons operate as separate platoons, each with their own Command team.

Your cavalrymen are fighting for their lives in the Losheim Gap. Their excellent training and hard work are helping to stem the tide of the German onslaught.

WEAPONS PLATOONS

Assault Gun Battery
Platoon

6 M8 Scott HMC	270 points	210 points
4 M8 Scott HMC	180 points	140 points
2 M8 Scott HMC	90 points	70 points

The assault guns of E Troop of the 32nd Cavalry Squadron were the first to respond to your cavalrymen's call for reinforcements. Tie them into your artillery network to add their guns to the corps' harassing bombardments.

LIEUTENANT
- Command M8 Scott HMC
- M8 Scott HMC
- M8 Scott HMC

HQ SECTION

SERGEANT
- M8 Scott HMC
- M8 Scott HMC
- M8 Scott HMC

GUN SECTION
ASSAULT GUN BATTERY

LIGHT TANK COMPANY
TANK COMPANY

MOTIVATION AND SKILL

A Light Tank Company from the 2nd Cavalry Group is rated **Confident Veteran**.

A Light Tank Company from the 14th Cavalry Group is rated **Confident Trained**.

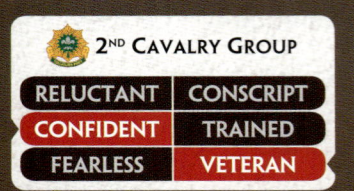

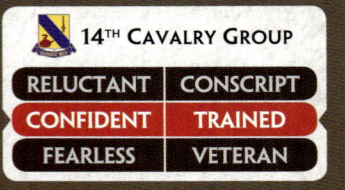

2ND CAVALRY GROUP
RELUCTANT	CONSCRIPT
CONFIDENT	TRAINED
FEARLESS	VETERAN

14TH CAVALRY GROUP
RELUCTANT	CONSCRIPT
CONFIDENT	TRAINED
FEARLESS	VETERAN

HEADQUARTERS

HEADQUARTERS
- Light Tank Company HQ (67)

You must field one platoon from each box shaded black and may field one platoon from each box shaded grey.

Your Company HQ must be either from the 2nd Cavalry Group (marked 🛡) or the 14th Cavalry Group (marked 🛡). All Combat and Weapons platoons marked with either of these symbols must be from the same cavalry group as your Company HQ. Support platoons can be of any variant type and do not have to match your Company HQ.

COMBAT PLATOONS

ARMOUR
- Light Tank Platoon (67)

ARMOUR
- Light Tank Platoon (67)

ARMOUR
- Light Tank Platoon (67)

WEAPONS PLATOONS

RECONNAISSANCE
- Cavalry Recon Platoon (65)

RECONNAISSANCE
- Cavalry Recon Platoon (65)

ARTILLERY
- Assault Gun Battery (65)

SUPPORT PLATOONS

ARMOUR OR ANTI-TANK
- Tank Destroyer Platoon (69)
- Towed Tank Destroyer Platoon (69)

INFANTRY
- Rifle Platoon (49)
- Armored Rifle Platoon (70)
- Engineer Combat Platoon (59)

ARTILLERY
- Field Artillery Battery (72)
- Armored Field Artillery Battery (74)
- Provisional Artillery Battery (73)

ARTILLERY
- Armored Field Artillery Battery (74)

AIRCRAFT
- Air Support (77)
- Air Observation Post (77)

LIGHT TANK COMPANY

HEADQUARTERS

LIGHT TANK COMPANY HQ

HEADQUARTERS

Company HQ with:

2 M24 Chaffee	165 points	130 points
2 M5A1 Stuart	105 points	80 points

OPTION
- Add M31 TRV recovery vehicle for +10 points or M32 TRV recovery vehicle for +15 points.

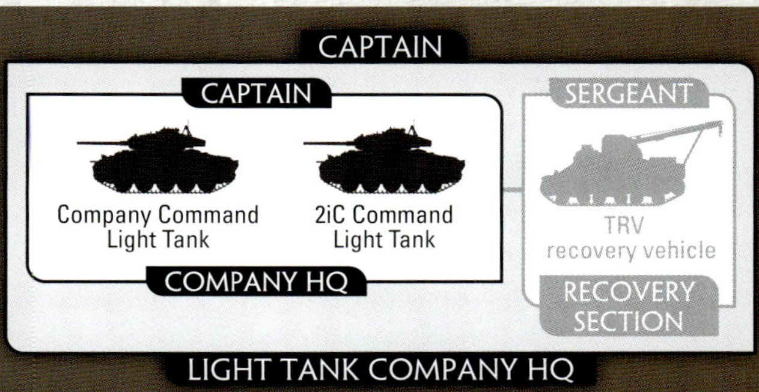

You must field at least one Light Tank Platoon entirely equipped with the same model of tank as the Light Tank Company HQ.

LIGHT TANK COMPANY HQ

- CAPTAIN — Company Command Light Tank
- CAPTAIN — 2iC Command Light Tank
- COMPANY HQ
- SERGEANT — TRV recovery vehicle — RECOVERY SECTION

F Troop is a light tank company under a different name. Armed with M5A1 Stuart (still called a the M3 by old hands), or the new M24 Chaffee, the troop's high speed allows them to keep up with the cavalry and lend support where needed.

COMBAT PLATOONS

LIGHT TANK PLATOON

PLATOON

5 M24 Chaffee	415 points	320 points
4 M24 Chaffee	335 points	255 points
3 M24 Chaffee	250 points	190 points
5 M5A1 Stuart	260 points	200 points
4 M5A1 Stuart	210 points	160 points
3 M5A1 Stuart	155 points	120 points

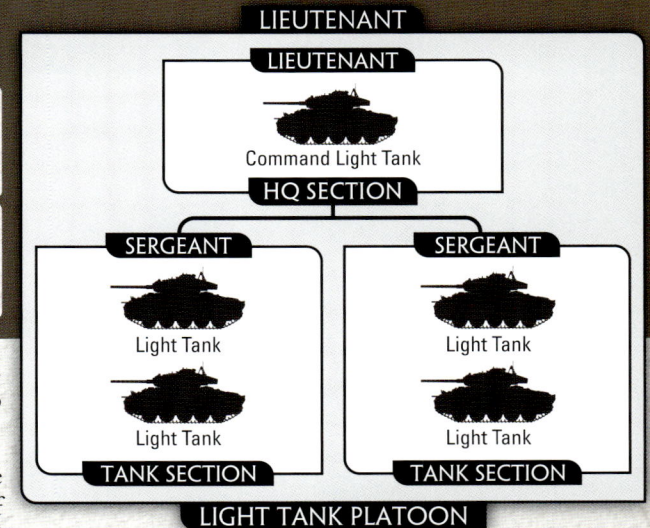

LIGHT TANK PLATOON

- LIEUTENANT — Command Light Tank — HQ SECTION
- SERGEANT — Light Tank, Light Tank — TANK SECTION
- SERGEANT — Light Tank, Light Tank — TANK SECTION

The light tanks of F Troop are usually the M5A1 Stuart. While a tried and true model, the tank has been relegated to specialist missions where they can exploit gaps in the line.

The new M24 Chaffee is an excellent replacement for the M5A1. It combines a powerful 75mm gun with the speed of a light tank, making it a deadly new weapon in the Arsenal of Freedom.

67

US SUPPORT

MOTIVATION AND SKILL

Fuel shortages and narrow attack corridors saw the armoured divisions work quite closely with a wide variety of infantry divisions, some experienced combat veterans, others fresh from the States.

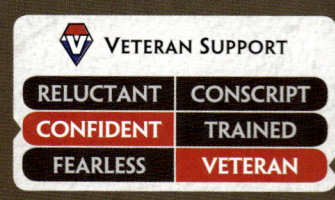

Veteran Support

RELUCTANT	CONSCRIPT
CONFIDENT	TRAINED
FEARLESS	**VETERAN**

Trained Support

RELUCTANT	CONSCRIPT
CONFIDENT	**TRAINED**
FEARLESS	VETERAN

TANK PLATOON

PLATOON

	V	T
5 M4 or M4A1 Sherman	415 points	320 points
4 M4 or M4A1 Sherman	335 points	255 points
3 M4 or M4A1 Sherman	250 points	190 points
5 M4A3 (76mm)	690 points	545 points
4 M4A3 (76mm)	555 points	435 points
3 M4A3 (76mm)	415 points	325 points

OPTION

- Fit any or all tanks with Improvised Armour for +5 points per tank.

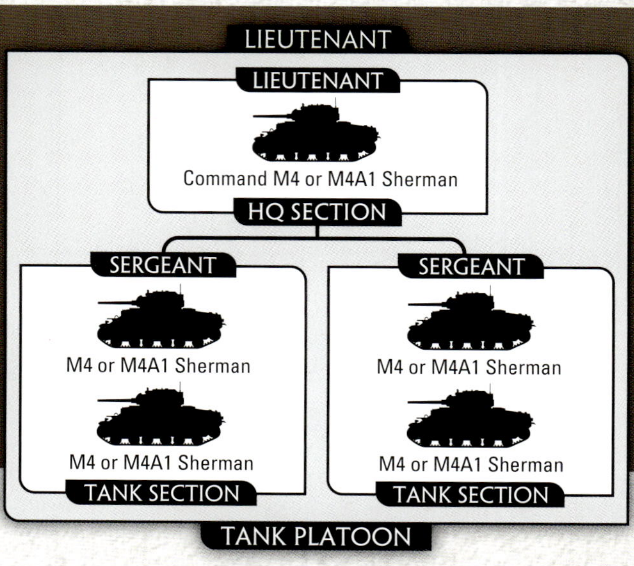

LIEUTENANT
Command M4 or M4A1 Sherman
HQ SECTION

SERGEANT
M4 or M4A1 Sherman
M4 or M4A1 Sherman
TANK SECTION

SERGEANT
M4 or M4A1 Sherman
M4 or M4A1 Sherman
TANK SECTION

TANK PLATOON

By the end of November 1944, several infantry-support battalions are fully equipped with 76mm versions, while others prefer the 75mm versions (especially the updates ones with better ammunition stowage) supported by a few specialist tanks, such as the Jumbo.

SHERMAN TANK UPGRADES

You can upgrade your M4 or M4A1 Sherman tanks from the Tank Platoons to newer models. For each tank you wish to upgrade, simply add the points (found to the right) that match the skill rating of the Tank Platoon you have chosen (V or T) to the cost of the platoon.

For example, in your full-strength Veteran (marked V) Tank Platoon (415 points), you would like to upgrade one tank to an M4A3E2 Jumbo, two tanks to M4A3 (76mm), and leave the rest as normal. This adds +60 for the Jumbo upgrade and +55 for each of the 76mm upgrades, for a total cost of 585 points for the platoon.

Replace one M4 or M4A1 tank with:	V	T
M4A3E2 Jumbo	+60 points	+50 points

Replace any or all M4 or M4A1 tanks with:	V	T
M4A3	+5 points	+5 points
M4A3 (late)	+20 points	+15 points

Replace up to two M4 or M4A1 tanks with:	V	T
M4A1 (76mm) (late)	+50 points	+40 points
M4A3 (76mm)	+55 points	+45 points

US SUPPORT

TANK DESTROYER PLATOON

PLATOON

Security Section and
Tank Destroyer Section with:

4 M36 90mm GMC	485 points	370 points
2 M36 90mm GMC	265 points	205 points
4 M18 Hellcat (late)	410 points	315 points
2 M18 Hellcat (late)	230 points	180 points
4 M10 3in GMC (late)	405 points	310 points
2 M10 3in GMC (late)	225 points	175 points

OPTIONS

- Replace any or all M10 3in GMC (late) tank destroyers with M36 90mm GMC tank destroyers for +20 points per tank destroyer.
- Replace any or all M10 3in GMC (late) tank destroyers with M36 90mm GMC tank destroyers for +15 points per tank destroyer. 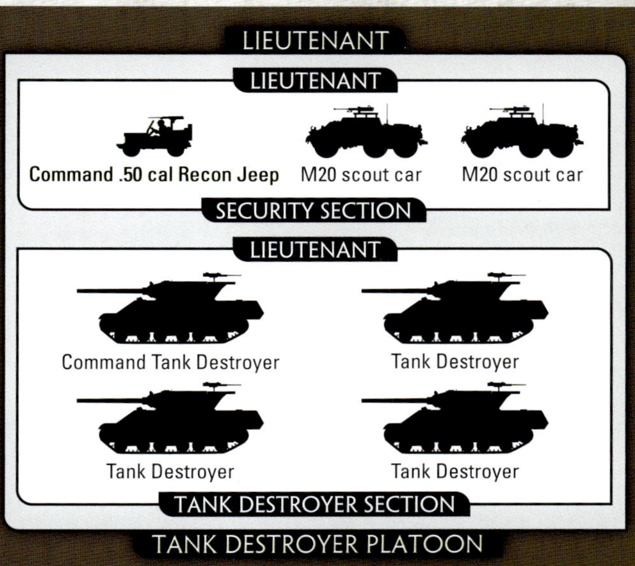
- Fit any or all tank destroyers with Improvised Armour for +5 points per tank.
- Upgrade all M10 3in GMC (late) tank destroyers with Top Armour 1 for +5 points per tank.

Tank Destroyer Platoons use the US Tank Destroyers special rules on page 238 of the rulebook.

A Tank Destroyer Platoon is a Reconnaissance Platoon.

LIEUTENANT
Command .50 cal Recon Jeep — M20 scout car — M20 scout car
SECURITY SECTION

LIEUTENANT
Command Tank Destroyer — Tank Destroyer
Tank Destroyer — Tank Destroyer
TANK DESTROYER SECTION

TANK DESTROYER PLATOON

TOWED TANK DESTROYER PLATOON

PLATOON

Security Section and Tank Destroyer Section with:

4 M5 3in (late)	255 points	195 points
2 M5 3in (late)	145 points	110 points

OPTIONS

- Add up to one Bazooka team per M5 3in (late) gun for +20 points per Bazooka team.
- Add up to one Bazooka team per M5 3in (late) gun for +15 points per Bazooka team.
- Add one M3 half-track per M5 3in gun for +5 points per half-track.

Towed Tank Destroyer Platoons use the US Tank Destroyers special rules on page 238 of the rulebook.

Few infantry divisions are supported by self-propelled tank destroyers. Instead they can rely on the heavy-hitting firepower of the towed M5 3in guns. These gunners have been specially trained to offer your GIs the best anti-tank coverage available.

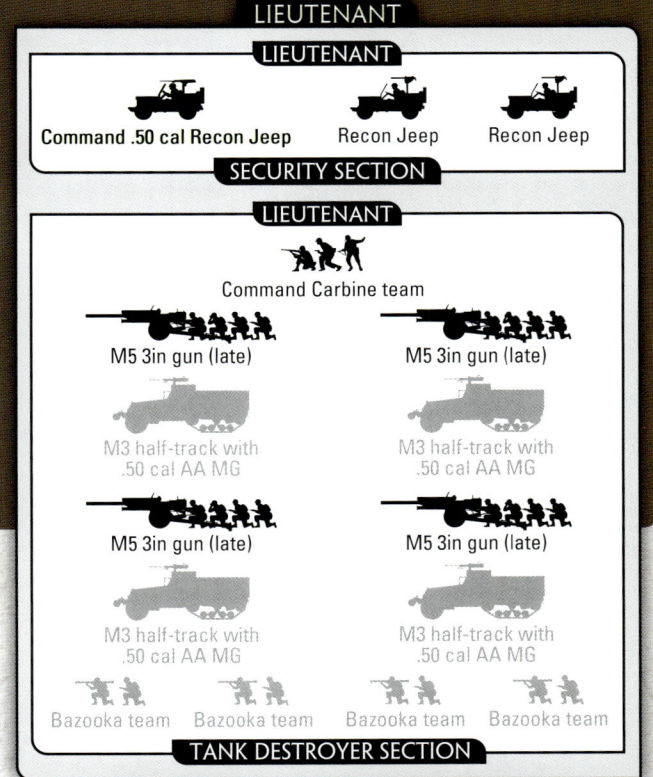

LIEUTENANT
Command .50 cal Recon Jeep — Recon Jeep — Recon Jeep
SECURITY SECTION

LIEUTENANT
Command Carbine team
M5 3in gun (late) — M5 3in gun (late)
M3 half-track with .50 cal AA MG — M3 half-track with .50 cal AA MG
M5 3in gun (late) — M5 3in gun (late)
M3 half-track with .50 cal AA MG — M3 half-track with .50 cal AA MG
Bazooka team — Bazooka team — Bazooka team — Bazooka team
TANK DESTROYER SECTION

TOWED TANK DESTROYER PLATOON

69

Armored Rifle Platoon

Platoon

HQ Section with
Light Machine-gun Squad,
60mm Mortar Squad, and:

2 Rifle Squads	225 points
1 Rifle Squads	180 points

Option

- Replace Bazooka team in HQ Section with an M3 37mm gun at no cost.

The arrival of the independent 526th Armored Rifle Battalion gives you the option to have an excellent mobile reserve backed by a tremendous amount of firepower. Send these armoured boys to where they are needed most, taking full advantage of their mobility. The fact that they are essentially an army unto themselves, with machine-guns, bazookas, and a mortar, means that you can rely on them to get the job done.

LIEUTENANT
LIEUTENANT — Command Rifle team, Rifle team, Bazooka team, M3 half-track with .50 cal AA MG

HQ SECTION

SERGEANT — Rifle team, Rifle team, M3 half-track with AA MG, Bazooka team
RIFLE SQUAD

SERGEANT — Rifle team, Rifle team, M3 half-track with AA MG, Bazooka team
RIFLE SQUAD

SERGEANT — M2 60mm mortar, M3 half-track with AA MG, Bazooka team
60MM MORTAR SQUAD

SERGEANT — M1919 LMG, M1919 LMG, M3 half-track with .50 cal AA MG, Bazooka team
LIGHT MACHINE-GUN SQUAD

ARMORED RIFLE PLATOON

Armored Anti-tank Platoon

Platoon

HQ Section with:

3 Gun Sections	100 points
2 Gun Sections	65 points

Option

- Add a Bazooka team to any or all Gun Sections for +15 points per Bazooka team.

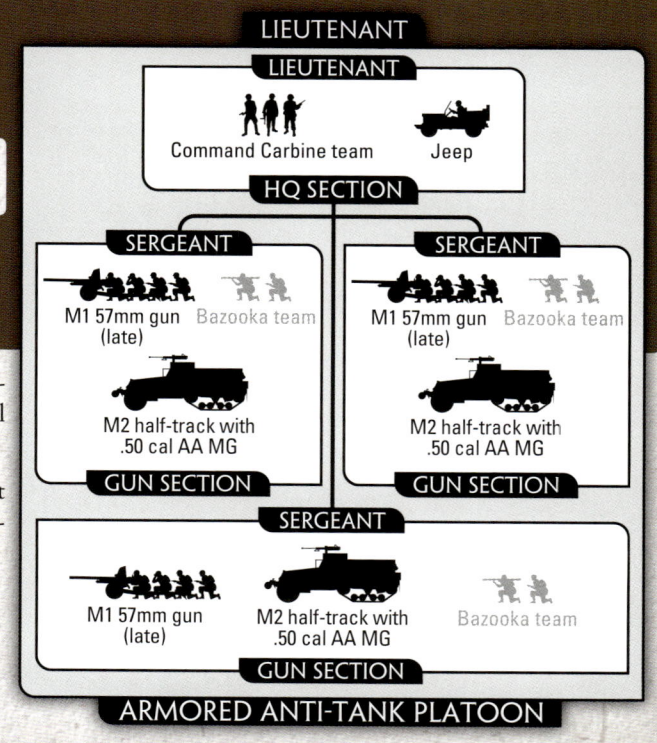

The 526th armoured rifles have also brought their own anti-tank guns with them. This added firepower will be essential as you setup your defences against the German attack.

The platoon's armoured half-tracks are also an essential aspect of your defence, offering their .50 cal anti-aircraft machine-guns to your troops.

LIEUTENANT
LIEUTENANT — Command Carbine team, Jeep

HQ SECTION

SERGEANT — M1 57mm gun (late), Bazooka team, M2 half-track with .50 cal AA MG
GUN SECTION

SERGEANT — M1 57mm gun (late), Bazooka team, M2 half-track with .50 cal AA MG
GUN SECTION

SERGEANT — M1 57mm gun (late), M2 half-track with .50 cal AA MG, Bazooka team
GUN SECTION

ARMORED ANTI-TANK PLATOON

US SUPPORT

PARACHUTE RIFLE PLATOON

PLATOON

HQ Section and Mortar Squad with:

3 Rifle Squads	265 points
2 Rifle Squads	205 points

*A Parachute Rifle Platoon is rated **Fearless Veteran**.*   **FEARLESS | VETERAN**

GAMMON BOMBS

All Rifle/MG teams in a Parachute Rifle Platoon carry Gammon Bombs giving them Tank Assault 3.

MASTER SERGEANT

Parachute missions are tricky and the loss of an officer can result in the failure of the mission. Therefore platoon sergeants are briefed on every detail of the mission in the event their officer is separated from the platoon.

Parachute Rifle Platoons use the German Mission Tactics special rules (see page 242 of the rulebook).

LIEUTENANT
- Command Rifle/MG team
- HQ SECTION

SERGEANT — Rifle/MG team, Rifle/MG team — RIFLE SQUAD
SERGEANT — Rifle/MG team, Rifle/MG team — RIFLE SQUAD
SERGEANT — Rifle/MG team, Rifle/MG team — RIFLE SQUAD
CORPORAL — M2 60mm Mortar, Bazooka team — MORTAR SQUAD

PARACHUTE RIFLE PLATOON

Among the first of the divisions to be rushed to the front is the highly-professional 82nd 'All American' Airborne Division. It has been called up from resting after the Market Garden battles to form the back-stop from Trois Ponts to Saint Vith. Meanwhile, the 101st 'Screaming Eagles' Airborne Division has been sent south to reinforce Bastogne. Whatever division these boys come from, these tough paratroopers will fight hard down to the last man.

Field Artillery Battery
Platoon

HQ Section with:

		V	T
4 M2A1 105mm		185 points	140 points
2 M2A1 105mm		100 points	75 points

Option
- Add ¾-ton and 2½-ton trucks for +5 points for the battery.

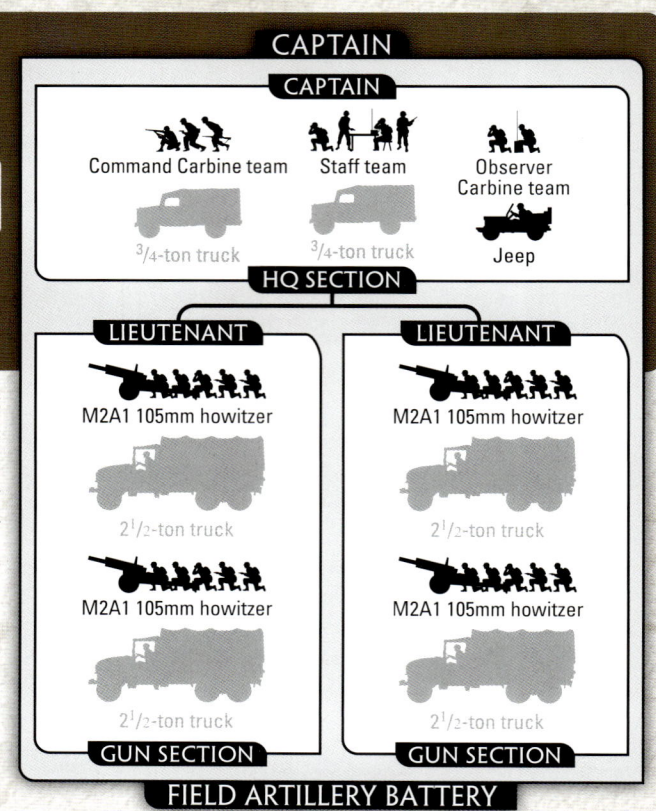

The US artillery arm deserves special attention for its valiant efforts in the Battle of the Bulge. Their ready and accurate fire missions repelled attempt after attempt to capture critical pieces of terrain, such as the Elsenborn Ridge. Without their rapid and devastating response, the Germans could easily have overrun the front lines.

Proximity Fuses
The US artillery used the new top secret proximity fuses for the first time in the Ardennes. These fuses would trigger an incoming shell to explode a few meters above the ground, scattering shrapnel over a much wider area than traditional shells. These new shells made the standard Time on Target easier for the gunners, and the overall effect was pandemonium among the German troops as they tried in vain to push forward.

CAPTAIN
- Command Carbine team — ¾-ton truck
- Staff team — ¾-ton truck
- Observer Carbine team — Jeep

HQ SECTION

LIEUTENANT
- M2A1 105mm howitzer — 2½-ton truck
- M2A1 105mm howitzer — 2½-ton truck

GUN SECTION

LIEUTENANT
- M2A1 105mm howitzer — 2½-ton truck
- M2A1 105mm howitzer — 2½-ton truck

GUN SECTION

FIELD ARTILLERY BATTERY

Field Artillery Battery (155mm)
Platoon

HQ Section with:

		V	T
4 M1 155mm		275 points	210 points
2 M1 155mm		145 points	110 points
4 M1A1 Long Tom		325 points	250 points
2 M1A1 Long Tom		175 points	130 points

Options
- Add ¾-ton trucks and M5 high-speed tractors for +5 points for the battery.
- Arm any or all M5 high-speed tractors with a .50 cal AA MG for +5 points per tractor.

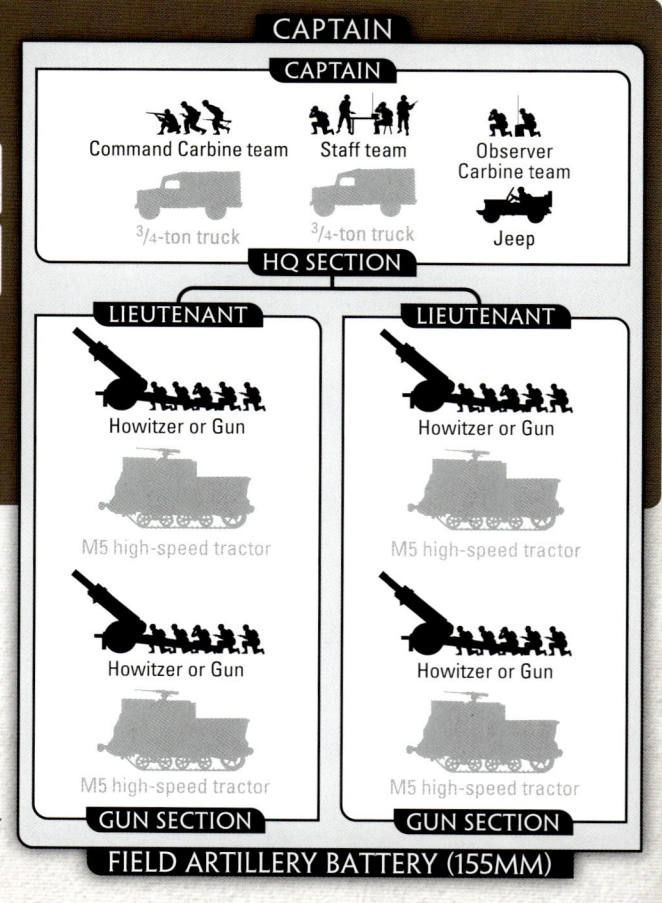

More often than you'd think, the brave artillerymen find themselves under fire from German tanks and infantry as they engage in a brutal point-blank fight. So dedicated are the artillerymen that they will see off the Germans or die beside their guns.

Isolated batteries of shattered divisions, and bypassed corps assets, such as the formidable M1A1 155mm 'Long Tom' guns fight on until they are out of ammunition. Even then the men spike their guns, pick up their rifles, and join the first US platoon they meet to do their part in the defence of the 'bulge'.

CAPTAIN
- Command Carbine team — ¾-ton truck
- Staff team — ¾-ton truck
- Observer Carbine team — Jeep

HQ SECTION

LIEUTENANT
- Howitzer or Gun — M5 high-speed tractor
- Howitzer or Gun — M5 high-speed tractor

GUN SECTION

LIEUTENANT
- Howitzer or Gun — M5 high-speed tractor
- Howitzer or Gun — M5 high-speed tractor

GUN SECTION

FIELD ARTILLERY BATTERY (155MM)

US SUPPORT

PROVISIONAL FIELD ARTILLERY BATTERY

PLATOON

HQ Section with:

4 8.8cm FlaK36	180 points
2 8.8cm FlaK36	95 points
4 8.8cm PaK 43/41	245 points
2 8.8cm PaK 43/41	130 points
4 8.8cm PaK 43	250 points
2 8.8cm PaK 43	135 points
4 10.5cm leFH18	135 points
2 10.5cm leFH18	75 points
4 122mm obr 1938	150 points
2 122mm obr 1938	85 points
4 15cm sFH18	210 points
2 15cm sFH18	110 points

OPTIONS

- Add ¾-ton trucks and M5 high-speed tractors for +5 points for the battery, or add ¾-ton trucks and Captured Sd Kfz 251/1 D half-tracks for +10 points for the battery.
- Arm any or all M5 high-speed tractors with a .50 cal AA MG for +5 points per tractor.

PROVISIONAL FIELD ARTILLERY BATTERY

- CAPTAIN
  - Command Carbine team (¾-ton truck)
  - Staff team (¾-ton truck)
  - Observer Carbine team (Jeep)
- HQ SECTION
- LIEUTENANT
  - Gun or Howitzer
  - Tractor of Half-track
  - Gun or Howitzer
  - Tractor of Half-track
- GUN SECTION
- LIEUTENANT
  - Gun or Howitzer
  - Tractor of Half-track
  - Gun or Howitzer
  - Tractor of Half-track
- GUN SECTION

After the hard fighting of Normandy the US Army is desperately short of 105mm ammunition. The solution was presented in the Field Artillery Journal in March 1945:

"In their haste to put the Siegfried Line between themselves and us, the Jerries have left a lot of shootable artillery pieces behind. Therefore, don't be surprised if your Division Ordnance Officer proudly presents you with a battery of captured material.

With that battery you will, if you are lucky, get one grimy tabular firing table and an unlimited supply of ammunition. The chief difficulty will be that no one knows whether the firing table applies to the weapon or whether the ammunition is the right type for the weapon or whether the firing table applies to the ammunition. You figure those simple things out for yourself.

The best way to answer all questions is to load the most likely-looking projectile ahead of the biggest bag of powder at the maximum elevation, then tie on your longest lanyard, put everybody in their deepest fox holes, and pull. If she goes off, and hangs together, and the infantry doesn't report a short round, you have a new battery all your own."

CAPTURED EQUIPMENT

The crews of the captured guns could not fire Time On Target bombardments with the unfamiliar guns and howitzers.

A Provisional Field Artillery Battery does not use the Time On Target special rule.

Armored Field Artillery Battery

Platoon

HQ Section with:

6 M7 Priest GMC	390 points	300 points
4 M7 Priest GMC	280 points	215 points
3 M7 Priest GMC	220 points	170 points

Options
- Add a Jeep and an M2 half-track with .50 cal AA MG for +5 points for the battery.
- Replace Jeep with an M2 half-track with AA MG for +5 points.

The M7 Priest is an armoured self-propelled 105mm howitzer. This gives the battery the ability to rush to where its needed and quickly put down a bombardment without having to unlimber, setup gun pits, and other cumbersome tasks of the towed artillery.

The 4th Infantry Division was unique in that they had batteries of four M7 Priests instead of towed guns. This stems from the division's history as the army's only mechanised division.

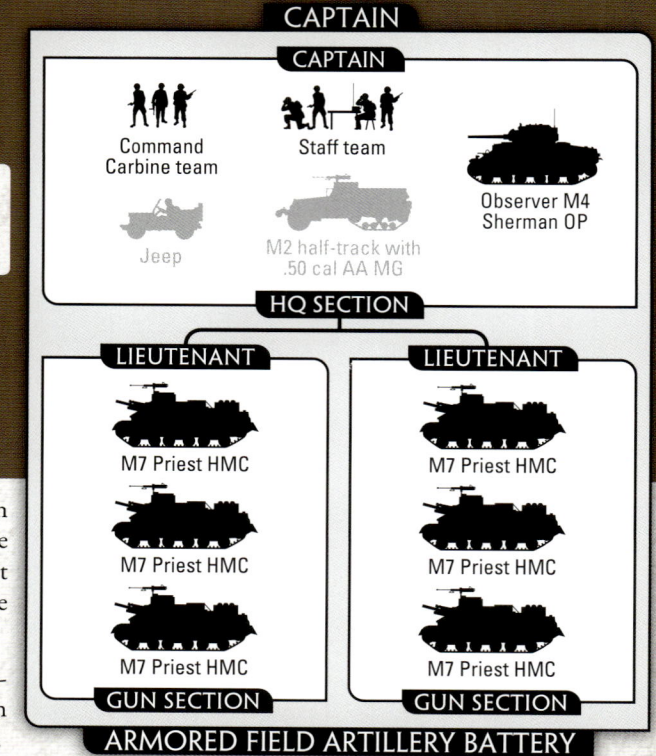

CAPTAIN

CAPTAIN
- Command Carbine team
- Staff team
- Observer M4 Sherman OP
- Jeep
- M2 half-track with .50 cal AA MG

HQ SECTION

LIEUTENANT
- M7 Priest HMC
- M7 Priest HMC
- M7 Priest HMC

GUN SECTION

LIEUTENANT
- M7 Priest HMC
- M7 Priest HMC
- M7 Priest HMC

GUN SECTION

ARMORED FIELD ARTILLERY BATTERY

ROCKET LAUNCHER BATTERY
PLATOON

HQ Section with:		
4 T27 Xylophone		135 points
2 T27 Xylophone		75 points

OPTION
- Model T27 Xylophone rocket launchers with five or more crew and count each rocket launcher as two weapons when firing a bombardment for +5 points per rocket launcher.
- Add a Jeep and a ¾-ton truck for +5 points for the battery.

The 2nd Infantry Division was the first to experiment with the T27 4.5" (114mm) Xylophone rocket launcher during the battle of Brest in August 1944. They rated them poorly because they were not effective as single launchers. To fix this, the artillerymen have paired up the launchers and put them on the back of a 2½-ton truck for better mobility and stronger bombardments.

ROCKET LAUNCHER BATTERY
- CAPTAIN — HQ SECTION: Command Carbine team, ¾-ton truck, Observer Carbine team, Jeep
- LIEUTENANT — GUN SECTION: T27 Xylophone, T27 Xylophone
- LIEUTENANT — GUN SECTION: T27 Xylophone, T27 Xylophone

ARMORED FIELD ARTILLERY BATTERY (155)
PLATOON

HQ Section with:		
4 M12 155mm GMC	335 points	260 points
2 M12 155mm GMC	180 points	135 points

OPTION
- Add ¾-ton trucks for +5 points for the battery.

You may not field an Armored Field Artillery Battery (155) unless you are also fielding a Field Artillery Battery or a Provisional Artillery Battery with at least as many Artillery teams.

The powerful M12 155mm self-propelled gun was used against the Siegfried Line, a job they had been well prepared for during the siege of Brest earlier. Now, during this battle, they are helping to shatter the German spearheads.

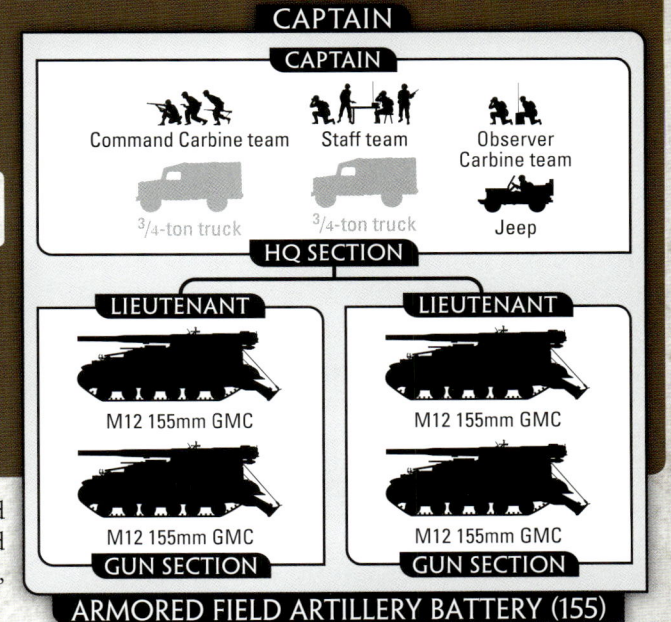

ARMORED FIELD ARTILLERY BATTERY (155)
- CAPTAIN — HQ SECTION: Command Carbine team (¾-ton truck), Staff team (¾-ton truck), Observer Carbine team (Jeep)
- LIEUTENANT — GUN SECTION: M12 155mm GMC, M12 155mm GMC
- LIEUTENANT — GUN SECTION: M12 155mm GMC, M12 155mm GMC

US SUPPORT

ANTI-AIRCRAFT ARTILLERY PLATOON

PLATOON

HQ Section with:

	V	T
2 M1 Bofors and 2 M49 quad .50 cal AA	120 points	90 points
1 M1 Bofors and 1 M49 quad .50 cal AA	60 points	45 points
2 M1 Bofors and 2 M2 .50 cal AA	90 points	70 points
1 M1 Bofors and 1 M2 .50 cal AA	45 points	35 points

OPTION
- Add Jeep and 2½-ton trucks for +5 points for the platoon.

M2 .50 cal AA guns are carried Portee on their trucks counting as a Tank team.

The high rate of fire heroic anti-aircraft gunners keeps the enemy aircraft away while the GIs rebuild a new defensive line.

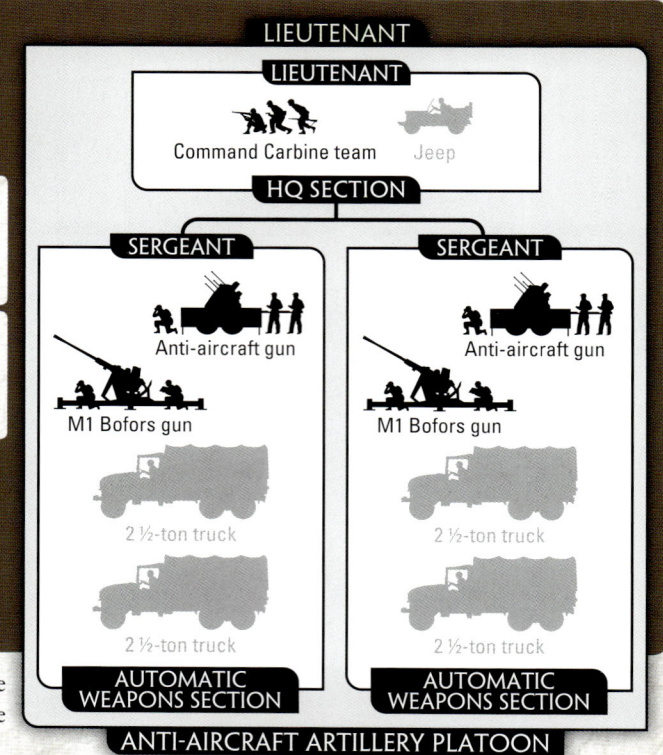

ANTI-AIRCRAFT ARTILLERY PLATOON

LIEUTENANT — Command Carbine team, Jeep
HQ SECTION

SERGEANT — Anti-aircraft gun, M1 Bofors gun, 2½-ton truck, 2½-ton truck — AUTOMATIC WEAPONS SECTION

SERGEANT — Anti-aircraft gun, M1 Bofors gun, 2½-ton truck, 2½-ton truck — AUTOMATIC WEAPONS SECTION

HEAVY ANTI-AIRCRAFT ARTILLERY PLATOON

PLATOON

HQ Section with:

	V	T
2 M1 90mm guns	160 points	120 points

OPTIONS
- Model M1 90mm Anti-aircraft gun with eight or more crew and increase their ROF to 3 for +10 points per gun.
- Add a Jeep and M5 high-speed tractors for +5 points for the platoon.
- Arm any or all M5 high-speed tractors with a .50 cal AA MG for +5 points per tractor.

The 49th Anti-Aircraft Artillery Brigade helped deal with Skorzeny's tanks when they attacked Malmédy.

HEAVY ANTI-AIRCRAFT ARTILLERY PLATOON

LIEUTENANT — Command Carbine team, Jeep
HQ SECTION

SERGEANT — M1 90mm gun, M5 high-speed tractor — ANTI-AIRCRAFT SECTION

SERGEANT — M1 90mm gun, M5 high-speed tractor — ANTI-AIRCRAFT SECTION

Anti-aircraft Artillery (self-propelled) Platoon

Platoon

	V	T
2 M16 MGMC (Quad .50 cal) and 2 M15 CGMC (37mm)	200 points	150 points
1 M16 MGMC (Quad .50 cal) and 1 M15 CGMC (37mm)	100 points	75 points

The self-propelled anti-aircraft half-tracks are excellent weapons to ambush the hapless *Volksgrenadiere* or clear enemy tanks of any passengers they might be carrying.

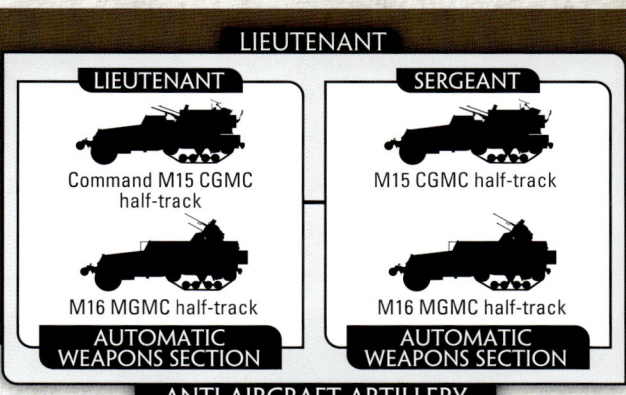

ANTI-AIRCRAFT ARTILLERY (SELF-PROPELLED) PLATOON

LIEUTENANT

- LIEUTENANT — Command M15 CGMC half-track
- SERGEANT — M15 CGMC half-track

AUTOMATIC WEAPONS SECTION
- M16 MGMC half-track

AUTOMATIC WEAPONS SECTION
- M16 MGMC half-track

Air Support

Priority Air Support

P-47 Thunderbolt	190 points

Limited Air Support

P-47 Thunderbolt	150 points

Options
- Equip P-47 Thunderbolts with 5.5" HVAR rockets in addition to their normal weapons for +30 points.
- Establish Close Air Support for +25 points.

Close Air Support

When the weather finally cleared up later in December, the USAAF poured hundreds of sorties into the Ardennes. Some pilots even defied orders and took to the skies in bad weather to support their comrades on the ground.

If you establish Close Air Support (see the option for Priority Air Support above), you roll two dice on the How Many Aircraft Table and take the best result.

The 406th Fighter Group operating in the skies above Bastogne was the first to use the new 5.5" High Velocity Aircraft Rocket (HVAR), affectionately known as 'Holy Moses' by the crews. This rocket was definitely an improvement over the older, ineffective 4.5" ones used earlier. Each P-47 could carry four of these large rockets, *in addition* to two bombs and its eight .50 cal machine-guns!

AIR SUPPORT
FLIGHT LIEUTENANT — P-47 Thunderbolt — FLIGHT

Air Observation Post

AOP

L4 Grasshopper AOP	40 points

Wherever possible, the brave AOP pilots took to the skies in spite of an active *Luftwaffe*, to direct artillery bombardments on the German spearheads.

AIR OBSERVATION POST
FLIGHT LIEUTENANT — L4 Grasshopper AOP — AOP

US ARSENAL

TANK TEAMS

Name *Weapon*	Mobility *Range*	Front *ROF*	Armour Side *Anti-tank*	Top *Firepower*	Equipment and Notes
LIGHT TANKS					
M5A1 Stuart	Light Tank	4	2	1	Co-ax MG, Hull MG, AA MG.
M6 37mm gun	*24"/60cm*	*2*	*7*	*4+*	*Stabiliser.*
M24 Chaffee	Light Tank	4	2	1	Co-ax MG, Hull MG, .50 cal AA MG.
M6 75mm gun	*32"/80cm*	*2*	*10*	*3+*	*Smoke, Stabiliser.*
TANKS					
M4 or M4A1 Sherman	Standard Tank	6	4	1	Co-ax MG, Hull MG, .50 cal AA MG, Tank telephone.
M3 75mm gun	*32"/80cm*	*2*	*10*	*3+*	*Smoke, Stabiliser.*
M4A3 Sherman	Standard Tank	6	4	1	Co-ax MG, Hull MG, .50 cal AA MG, Detroit's finest, Tank telephone.
M3 75mm gun	*32"/80cm*	*2*	*10*	*3+*	*Smoke, Stabiliser.*
M4A3 Sherman (late)	Standard Tank	7	4	1	Co-ax MG, Hull MG, .50 cal AA MG, Detroit's finest, Protected ammo, Tank telephone.
M3 75mm gun	*32"/80cm*	*2*	*10*	*3+*	*Smoke, Stabiliser.*
M4A1 (76mm) Sherman (late)	Standard Tank	7	4	1	Co-ax MG, Hull MG, .50 cal AA MG, Protected ammo, Tank telephone.
M1 76mm gun (late)	*32"/80cm*	*2*	*13*	*3+*	*Stabiliser.*
M4A3 (76mm) Sherman	Standard Tank	7	4	1	Co-ax MG, Hull MG, .50 cal AA MG, Detroit's finest, Protected ammo, Tank telephone.
M1 76mm gun (late)	*32"/80cm*	*2*	*13*	*3+*	*Stabiliser.*
M4A3E2 Jumbo	Slow Tank	12	8	1	Co-ax MG, Hull MG, .50 cal AA MG, Jumbos lead the way, Tank telephone.
M3 75mm gun	*32"/80cm*	*2*	*10*	*3+*	*Smoke, Stabiliser.*

SHERMAN TANK SPECIAL RULES

DETROIT'S FINEST

Tanks that use the Detroit's Finest special rule have a Movement Distance of 14"/35cm on Roads or Cross-country Terrain.

DUCKBILLS

At the start of the game a player may elect to fit all of their tanks from the following list with Duckbills:

- Sherman (all variants)
- M7 Priest HMC
- M12 155mm GMC
- M10 3" GMC (late)
- M36 90mm GMC
- T34 Calliope

This gives them Wide Tracks (see page 61 of the rulebook), but makes their mobility rating Slow Tank.

M4A3E2 Jumbo, M18 76mm GMC, M24 Chaffee, M5A1 Stuart, and M8 Scott HMC tanks cannot be fitted with Duckbills and ignore the Duckbills special rule.

JUMBOS LEAD THE WAY

You may allocate hits to an M4A3E2 Jumbo tank as if it had the lowest armour rating, assigning it a hit before the lesser armoured tanks.

This rule does not apply to hits from Artillery Bombardments or hits from Aircraft.

TANK TELEPHONES

If a Tank team with Tank Telephone and an adjacent Infantry team did not move in the Movement Step, and the Infantry team is not Pinned Down, the Infantry team can use the Eyes and Ears rule (see page 195 of the rulebook) to Reveal one Gone to Ground enemy team to that Tank team as if the Infantry team was a Recce team. If other tanks in the platoon fire, they must either have their own Infantry team pointing out the target or continue to treat the target as Gone to Ground.

US ARSENAL

Tank Destroyers (Self-Propelled)

M10 3in GMC (late)	Standard Tank	4	2	0	.50 cal AA MG.
M7 3in gun (late)	*32"/80cm*	2	13	3+	*Slow traverse.*
M18 Hellcat (late)	Light Tank	2	0	0	.50 cal AA MG.
M1 76mm gun (late)	*32"/80cm*	2	13	3+	
M36 90mm GMC	Standard Tank	4	2	0	.50 cal AA MG, Detroit's finest.
M3 90mm gun	*32"/80cm*	2	14	3+	

Support Weapons

M8 Scott HMC	Light Tank	3	2	0	.50 cal AA MG.
M1A1 75mm howitzer	*16"/40cm*	2	6	3+	*Smoke.*
Firing bombardments	*64"/160cm*	-	3	6	
M4 (105mm) Sherman	Standard Tank	7	4	1	Co-ax MG, Hull MG, .50 cal AA MG, Protected ammo.
M4 105mm howitzer	*24"/60cm*	1	9	2+	*Breakthrough gun, Slow traverse, Smoke.*
Firing bombardments	*48"/120cm*	-	4	4+	
T34 Calliope	Standard Tank	6	4	1	Co-ax MG, Hull MG.
T34 Calliope rocket launcher	*48"/120cm*	-	2	5+	*Rocket launcher, Saturation Bombardment, Sixty Rockets.*

Artillery (Self-Propelled)

M7 Priest HMC	Standard Tank	1	0	0	.50 cal AA MG.
M2A1 105mm howitzer	*24"/60cm*	1	9	2+	*Hull mounted, Breakthrough gun, Smoke.*
Firing bombardments	*72"/180cm*	-	4	4+	*Smoke bombardment.*
M12 155mm GMC	Standard Tank	0	0	0	Awkward layout.
M1918M1 155mm gun	*24"/60cm*	1	13	1+	*Hull mounted, Bunker buster, Smoke.*
Firing bombardments	*96"/240cm*	-	5	2+	*Smoke bombardment.*
T27 Xylophone	Wheeled	-	-	-	.50 cal AA MG.
T27 rocket launcher	*48"/120cm*	-	2	5+	*Rocket launcher.*
M4 Sherman OP	Standard Tank	6	4	1	Co-ax MG, Hull MG, .50 cal AA MG.
M3 75mm gun	*32"/80cm*	1	10	3+	*Smoke.*

Anti-aircraft (Self Propelled)

M16 MGMC (Quad .50 cal)	Half-tracked	1	0	0	
M45 quad .50 cal gun	*16"/40cm*	6	4	5+	*Anti-aircraft.*
M15 CGMC (37mm)	Wheeled	1	0	0	
M15 37mm combination mount	*24"/60cm*	4	5	4+	*Anti-aircraft.*
M2 .50 cal AA on GMC	Wheeled	-	-	-	
M2 .50 cal AA gun	*16"/40cm*	4	4	5+	*Anti-aircraft, Portee.*

Reconnaissance

M8 armoured car	Wheeled	1	0	0	Co-ax MG, .50 cal AA MG, Recce.
M6 37mm gun	*24"/60cm*	2	7	4+	
M20 Scout car	Jeep	1	0	0	.50 cal AA MG, Recce.
Armored Recon Jeep	Jeep	0	0	0	AA MG, Overloaded, Recce.
Armored .50 Cal Recon Jeep	Jeep	0	0	0	.50 Cal AA MG, Overloaded, Recce.
Bazooka Recon Jeep	Jeep	0	0	0	Overloaded, Recce.
Twin M1 Bazooka launcher	*8"/20cm*	2	10	5+	*Hull mounted.*
Recon Jeep	Jeep	-	-	-	AA MG, Recce.
.50 cal Recon Jeep	Jeep	-	-	-	.50 Cal AA MG, Recce.
Mortar Jeep	Jeep	-	-	-	Recce.
M2 60mm mortar	*24"/60cm*	2	1	3+	*Hull mounted, Portee, Minimum range 8"/20cm.*
Firing Bombardments	*32"/80cm*	-	1	6	

Vehicle Machine-guns

Vehicle MG	16"/40cm	3	2	6	ROF 1 if other weapons fire.
.50 cal Vehicle MG	16"/40cm	3	4	5+	ROF 1 if other weapons fire.

GUN TEAMS

Weapon	Mobility	Range	ROF	Anti-tank	Firepower	Notes
M2 .50 cal MG	Man-packed	16"/40cm	3	4	5+	
M1919 LMG	Man-packed	16"/40cm	5	2	6	ROF 2 when Pinned Down or Moving.
M1917 HMG	Man-packed	24"/60cm	6	2	6	ROF 3 when Pinned Down or Moving.
M2 60mm mortar	Man-packed	24"/60cm	2	1	3+	Minimum range 8"/20cm.
Firing bombardments		32"/80cm	-	1	6	
M1 81mm mortar	Man-packed	24"/60cm	2	2	3+	Smoke, Minimum range 8"/20cm.
Firing bombardments		40"/100cm	-	2	6	Smoke bombardment.
4.2in Chemical mortar	Light	48"/120cm	-	3	4+	Smoke bombardment.
M2 .50 cal AA gun	Heavy	16"/40cm	4	4	5+	Anti-aircraft, Turntable.
M49 quad .50 cal AA gun	Heavy	16"/40cm	6	4	5+	Anti-aircraft, Turntable.
M1 Bofors gun	Immobile	24"/60cm	4	6	4+	Anti-aircraft, Turntable.
M1 90mm gun	Immobile	40"/100cm	2	13	3+	Heavy Anti-aircraft, Turntable.
M3 37mm gun	Light	24"/60cm	3	7	4+	Gun shield.
M1 57mm gun (late)	Medium	24"/60cm	3	10	4+	Gun shield.
M5 3in gun (late)	Immobile	32"/80cm	2	13	3+	Gun shield.
M3 105mm light howitzer	Heavy	16"/40cm	1	7	2+	Breakthrough gun, Smoke.
Firing bombardments		56"/140cm	-	4	4+	Smoke bombardment.
M2A1 105mm howitzer	Immobile	24"/60cm	1	9	2+	Breakthrough gun, Gun shield, Smoke.
Firing bombardments		72"/180cm	-	4	4+	Smoke bombardment.
M1 155mm howitzer	Immobile	24"/60cm	1	10	1+	Bunker buster, Gun shield, Smoke.
Firing bombardments		88"/220cm	-	5	2+	Smoke bombardment.
M1A1 Long Tom gun	Immobile	24"/60cm	1	13	1+	Bunker buster, Smoke.
Firing bombardments		104"/260cm	-	5	2+	Smoke bombardment.
8.8cm FlaK 36 gun	Immobile	40"/100cm	1	13	3+	Gun shield, Turntable.
Firing bombardments		88"/220cm	-	3	5+	
8.8cm PaK43/41 gun	Immobile	40"/100cm	1	16	3+	Gun shield.
Firing bombardments		88"/220cm	-	3	5+	
8.8cm PaK43 gun	Immobile	40"/100cm	1	16	3+	Gun shield, Turntable.
Firing bombardments		88"/220cm	-	3	5+	
10.5cm leFH18 howitzer	Immobile	24"/60cm	1	9	2+	Gun shield,
Firing bombardments		72"/180cm	-	4	4+	
122mm obr 1938	Immobile	24"/60cm	1	8	2+	Gun shield.
Firing bombardments		80"/200cm	-	4	3+	
15cm sFH18 howitzer	Immobile	24/60cm	1	11	1+	Bunker buster.
Firing bombardments		80"/200cm	-	5	2+	

US ARSENAL

FORTIFICATIONS

BUNKERS

Weapon	Range	ROF	Anti-tank	Firepower	Notes
.50 Cal Nest	16"/40cm	3	4	5+	

INFANTRY TEAMS

Team	Range	ROF	Anti-tank	Firepower	Notes
Carbine team	8"/20cm	1	1	6	Automatic rifles.
Rifle team	16"/40cm	1	2	6	Automatic rifles.
Rifle/MG team	16"/40cm	2	2	6	
SMG team	4"/10cm	3	1	6	Full ROF when moving.
Bazooka team	8"/20cm	1	10	5+	Tank assault 4.
Staff team	16"/40cm	1	2	6	Automatic rifles, Moves as a Heavy Gun team.

ADDITIONAL TRAINING AND EQUIPMENT

Pioneer teams and teams equipped with Gammon Bombs are rated as Tank Assault 3.

TRANSPORT TEAMS

Vehicle / Weapon	Mobility / Range	Front Armour / ROF	Side Armour / Anti-tank	Top Armour / Firepower	Equipment and Notes
TRUCKS					
Jeep or Captured Kübelwagen jeep	Jeep	-	-	-	Optional Passenger-fired AA MG or .50 cal AA MG.
Dodge ¾-ton, Dodge 1½-ton, or GMC 2½-ton truck	Wheeled	-	-	-	Optional Passenger-fired AA MG or .50 cal AA MG.
GMC 2½-ton dump truck	Wheeled	-	-	-	Optional Passenger-fired .50 cal AA MG.
Captured 3-ton truck	Wheeled	-	-	-	
M5 high-speed tractor	Standard Tank	-	-	-	Optional .50 cal AA MG.
ARMOURED PERSONNEL CARRIERS					
M2 or M3 half-track	Half-tracked	1	0	0	Optional Passenger-fired AA MG or .50 cal AA MG.
Captured Sd Kfz 251/1 D half-track	Half-tracked	1	0	0	Passenger-fired AA MG.
RECOVERY AND ENGINEER VEHICLES					
M31 TRV recovery vehicle	Standard Tank	5	3	0	Recovery vehicle.
M32 TRV recovery vehicle	Standard Tank	6	4	0	.50 cal AA MG, Recovery vehicle.
D7 Bulldozer	Very Slow Tank	0	0	0	Bulldozer.

AIRCRAFT

Aircraft	Weapon	To Hit	Anti-tank	Firepower	Notes
P-47 Thunderbolt	MG	2+	6	5+	
	Bombs	4+	5	1+	
	Rockets	3+	6	3+	Optional.

ARDENNES BATTLEFIELDS

The Ardennes region covers Luxembourg and portions of Belgium and France. For centuries it provided a physical barrier for invading armies between France and Germany. However, in 1940, the Germans launched an offensive through the Ardennes into France. The attack took the Allies completely by surprise and the Germans were able to envelop their enemy and ultimately achieve victory.

Four years later the Germans attempted the same thing, this time with the help of bad weather to hinder Allied air power. The thick woods of the Ardennes offered additional cover from the air as the columns moved through the region. However, the small roads and tracks of the Ardennes grew muddy and impassable, throwing the Germans' time table out the window.

To the men on the ground, the Ardennes was as difficult to contend with as the enemy, and as a result, the terrain played a decisive role in the battle.

CLEARINGS

Clearings weren't entirely uncommon in the Ardennes. The Losheim Gap got its name for being the only area through the Ardennes clear enough for armoured operations. Clearings are rated as cross-country terrain.

ROADS & TRACKS

In the Ardennes, roads typically ran north-to-south along the major rivers and the national borders. Narrow winding tracks linked the major roads together. Roads are rated as Roads, but tracks are rated as Cross-country terrain.

FORESTS

The Ardennes is a massive forested region, broken up in places by the occasional clearing. Large portions of the forest had been replanted in massive groves; the trees planted in long and precise rows with large gaps in between. The sandy soil of the northern forest prevents undergrowth, so it is easy to see long distances into the woods.

You can model this on your battlefield by covering a majority of your table with wooded areas. Rather than treating these forests as area terrain as usual, simply make the area they occupy conceal those teams inside. To represent the complications of manoeuvring vehicles in forests, they should be rated as Slow Going (rather than difficult or very difficult going as usual).

SIEGFRIED LINE OBSTACLES

Portions of the Ardennes were crossed by the formidable Siegfried Line, the large German network of fortifications stretching along the German border. These fortifications occasionally impacted the Ardennes fighting as large rows of Dragon's Teeth anti-tank obstacles crossed battlefields, frustrating German and American tanks alike.

You can model this on your Ardennes battlefield by adding a few lines of Barbed Wire, Minefields, or anti-tank Obstacles as terrain. Leave a few gaps here and there to make sure that you're not giving one side too great of an advantage!

ARDENNES BATTLEFIELDS

RUINED VILLAGES

As the Germans tore through the Ardennes, sometimes the only response available to the Americans was incessant artillery bombardments. These flattened villages and left them in ruin, offering the soldiers some improvised cover as the battles ebbed and flowed through the region.

When fighting over a ruined village, be sure to check out the rulebook for rules covering ruins and village buildings.

WRECKAGE AND BATTLEFIELD LITTER

The Battle of the Bulge produced a staggering amount of battlefield Wreckage and litter. *SS-Kampfgruppe* Peiper's column alone abandoned 31 tanks and 47 half-tracks in La Gleize when they headed back to German lines.

Feel free to model fields of wreckage, offering concealment for troops hiding within. Vehicles find the wreckage Slow Going when moving through it.

FUEL DUMPS

The Germans were always on the lookout for American Fuel dumps to keep their columns running. Fuel dumps make an excellent objective or centrepiece for your Ardennes battlefields.

CLEARING STATIONS

Throughout the Ardennes, medical clearing stations found themselves in the thick of the battle. These were a source of extra manpower, as officers patched together small platoons from the walking wounded to go out and help hold the line. Like fuel dumps, clearing stations make an excellent objective or centrepieces for your Ardennes battlefields.

STREAMS & RIVERS

Streams, canals, and small rivers flowed between the Meuse and Rhine rivers, creating a massive waterway network through the Ardennes. Streams are Difficult Going with Slow Going Fords where tracks cross. Rivers and canals are wider, and are Very Difficult Going.

FORDS AND BRIDGES

Fords and Bridges were vital objectives for armies moving across the Ardennes. Fords across Rivers are Difficult Going, but Bridges are rated as roads. For a bit of fun, feel free to use the optional Bridge Demolition special rules to represent old rickety structures and demolitions!

83

WINTER WEATHER

Perhaps the single most defining aspect of the Ardennes battles is the weather. Certainly the Germans knew that as they carefully planned the offensive during the time when the weather would ground Allied planes, allowing their panzers to travel in the daylight.

However, the bad weather was a double-edged sword as the freezing rain mixed with the mud to create terrible conditions on the roads. Deep snow piled up in the few clearings, making it tough for troops to slog their way through. The white snow blinded the troops as they kept a vigilant watch from their freezing foxholes.

What follows are several optional rules for representing bad weather in your games.

YOUR BATTLEFIELD

These rules are optional. Feel free to use all of them, but be aware that this can lead to slower and longer games.

If that isn't your style but you'd still like to add some flavour to your battle, go ahead and choose a few of the rules to use in your game and leave the others for another time and another battle.

OPTIONAL WINTER BATTLE SPECIAL RULES

SNOW-COVERED TERRAIN

Moving in the snow presents a lot of hazards to the unwary traveller. Deep snow impedes foot traffic as much as it does vehicle movement.

All teams treat snow-covered Roads as Cross-country Terrain, and all other snow-covered Terrain as Slow Going.

ICE

Packed snow and ice make moving vehicles a risky affair. Black ice, which is extremely hard to spot, especially, makes honest men out of even the most reckless drivers!

If a vehicle moves more than 8"/20cm in the Movement Step, at the end of its movement roll a Skill Check for that vehicle.

- *If successful, the vehicle navigates through the ice and carries on unharmed.*
- *Otherwise, the vehicle slips on the ice and becomes Bogged Down.*

FROZEN RIVERS AND PONDS

Frozen rivers, streams, lakes, and ponds posed their own threats, not the least of which was the temptation to cross them with armoured vehicles to bypass the destroyed bridges.

For light vehicles, such as trucks, jeeps, and other utility vehicles, a frozen river is easier to cross. For these vehicles a frozen river is rated as Cross-country terrain covered in Ice (see above).

However, a crossing is far more risky for armoured vehicles. When an Armoured vehicle attempts to cross a frozen river, it must roll a die and add 3 to the result.

- *If the total is less than the vehicle's Front armour, the ice gives way under the vehicle's weight and the vehicle is Destroyed.*
- *Otherwise the vehicle safely navigates the river and it may continue as normal.*

SNOW STORM

Snow storms were frequent in January 1945, and caused a bit of confusion and frustration.

If you and your opponent agree, your battle can take place during a snow storm. The game is played under the Night Fighting rules in the rulebook (see page 272 of the rulebook). The mission is played at Dawn (see page 273 of the rulebook).

BLIZZARD

Blizzards are a more serious breed of snow storm. They can strike suddenly, delivering a pile of snow within a matter of minutes.

If both players agree you can decide to have the potential of a blizzard strike your battlefield.

If a Blizzard could strike in your battle, roll a die at the start of each player's turn. On a 1, the blizzard strikes. That turn and those following are played under the Night Fighting rules in the rulebook (pages 272 and 273).

Instead of using the Night Visibility Table, use the Blizzard Visibility Table below to find out how far your teams can see in the Blizzard.

Players continue to roll at the start of their turn. On a 5+ the Blizzard dies off, and the rest of the game uses the normal visibility rules.

If the game is not already using the Snow-covered Terrain special rule when the Blizzard strikes, the rest of the game is played with them in effect.

BLIZZARD VISIBILITY TABLE

Dice Roll	Distance
1 or 2	4"/10cm
3 or 4	8"/20cm
5 or 6	12"/30 cm